YOUR DIVORCE

HANDBOOK

It's What You Do Next That Counts

GW00658338

Published by:
Stellar Books
1 Birchdale
St Mary's Road
Bowdon
Cheshire
WA14 2PW

www.stellarbooks.co.uk

ISBN: 978-1-910275-32-0

Published in 2021.

A catalogue record for this book is available at the British Library.

Designed and typeset in Calibri, Gill Sans MT by Stellar Books

FSC is a non-profit international organisation established to promote responsible management of the world's forests. Products carrying the FSC label are independently certified to assure consumers that they come from forests that are managed to meet the social economic and ecological needs of present and future generations.

YOUR DIVORCE HANDBOOK

It's What You Do Next That Counts

Tamsin Caine   Susan Leigh   Marcia Lister

Katie McCann   Carole Nettleton   Daniel Bell

STELLAR BOOKS

CONTENTS

INTRODUCTION

"HELP! We're separating (or have separated) and have no idea where to start." Are you feeling like this? You have suddenly been thrown into an unknown world that you need to negotiate so that you can move forward with your life. You probably feel fearful about money, where you will live and what will happen with the children, if you have them. You try to read up on what will happen and find a world full of jargon that you don't understand or guides that look like school textbooks!

Firstly, take a deep breath. You do not need to race to make any decisions. In fact, we would suggest that you begin by taking time to get some emotional help and support before you start making any big decisions.

You have taken the first step by buying this handbook. Within it, we will guide you through the options available to you whether you are divorcing or dissolving a civil partnership. The book has been written by a team of professionals who spend much of our working lives supporting people just like you. We will take you one step at a time through the process and the options you may have. We will also explain the legal and financial terms that you might need to understand.

Amicable – The absence of discord

There are two schools of thought when it comes to divorce: "Take them for everything they have" and "amicable resolution". You may be feeling anger and resentment towards the other person and wonder why you should possibly think about an amicable resolution. Alternatively, you may feel that you would like to move forward without any bitterness and want to pursue the best option without too much of a fight.

The authors of this handbook prefer to see couples resolve their issues without the need for court, preferably in an amicable way. The benefits of doing so enable you to move forward with your life more quickly, often with lower costs than the court options and with a greater chance that if you should need to be in contact with your ex in the future, it will be much less painful.

However, finding an amicable solution does not mean rolling over and letting your ex have everything their way either. We want you to find a FAIR solution, where both of you can move forward. The likelihood is that you will both have to compromise in order to find the best solution.

Splitting up is hard. Working out the fairest way to move forward, to separate the finances, and to agree arrangements for any children, is difficult and there is no straightforward formula that works for everyone. However, over the course of the next twelve chapters, we will guide you through the basics. Grab a cup of coffee and let's get started.

HOW TO USE THIS HANDBOOK

Those contemplating divorce often have many questions concerning their future choices and options, and even questions they don't know they should ask!

This handbook is not intended as a substitute for professional advice and input, but it has been collated by professionals to provide useful guidance and information at a time in life when you may need some friendly, supportive hand-holding.

It's not intended to be read straight through from beginning to end, although of course you can, but rather dipped into as and when required. Use the comprehensive index to guide you to where you need to be. There might be some slight duplication of content on occasion, as some situations warrant input from different specialisms.

There's a saying, 'It's not what happens to us in life that's significant, as much as how we respond and react. It's that which makes all the difference to our life, health and wellbeing.' This goal of this handbook is to ensure that you are fully equipped to deal with your divorce in an appropriate, informed and positive way.

If this sounds like you, then you're in exactly the right place.

Welcome.

*Breaking up can
be hard to do,
but don't let it define
you for the
rest of your days.*

1

DOES DIVORCE MEAN THAT I'M A FAILURE?

We've all learned from experience that relationships aren't easy. They require hard work to succeed, with long-timers frequently referencing their ups and downs with a wry smile, remembering how they couldn't envisage life without each other, planning their futures together, discussing children, travel and old age, musing over their many future possibilities with laughter and affection.

If that goes completely wrong, we may ask ourselves, what happened to all that love, what went wrong and resulted in us now getting divorced? Should we have tried harder, made more of an effort? Does divorce mean I'm a failure?

Reflections on why our relationship went so wrong

The run up to getting divorced is often a debilitating process, wearing us down, causing us to question and doubt ourselves. Over time we've shared an array of experiences, grown up together, loved each other. Recognising that things are deteriorating in our relationship can be a gradual process. We may still love them, but not in the way we know we should.

There's often much distress, confusion and recrimination as a relationship falls apart. Should we end it, are we doing the right thing, what if the grass is not greener elsewhere, are we making a mistake, will we ever find someone who cares for us as much as our partner did?

Yes, over the years we come to accept that change happens. Life brings different opportunities and challenges that may take us in unexpected directions, so opening up new choices, perspectives and priorities. Children, financial worries, health issues and the demands of family all bring additional pressures into our lives.

As a consequence, the things that initially attracted us to each other may have begun to irritate. The easy-going charmer may gradually be viewed as lazy and lacking in motivation. The person who's focused and career-driven may be regarded as a ruthless, money-obsessed workaholic. Qualities which, could in themselves be fine, may no longer be wanted in our lives.

When one person eventually says, 'Enough, this can't continue! It's time to go our separate ways', it's not a decision they've taken lightly. They may have repeatedly tried to rekindle the relationship, perhaps suggested relationship counselling in their desire to make it work. After all, they once cared deeply for their partner. But deciding to end a difficult and unhappy relationship often ultimately works out best for all concerned.

Breaking up can be hard to do!

It's not unusual for two people to have very different views on the state of their relationship. They may not be in the same place emotionally or one may simply refuse to accept that it's over. It may even be that one person feels everything's fine and perhaps hasn't noticed the cues from their partner that they're restless and wanting to move on. Breaking-up can be tough when we know the other person is heavily invested and is hanging on. Few of us want to be responsible for someone else's pain, especially when they were once such an important part of our lives.

- **Emotional and financial** considerations can influence the decision to break-up. Also, children may be a serious consideration: how disruptive will a break-up be, how much will it impact on their stability and wellbeing? Wider family implications can also factor: disappointing others, damaging the status quo. Complicated finances can all be enough to cause couples to stay together. Splitting the household, sorting out a settlement, agreeing custody as well as facing a large legal bill can be enough to deter some couples from breaking-up.

- **Secrets may well be a significant part** of the relationship. Caring deeply about someone includes sharing our innermost thoughts, fears and concerns, maybe disclosing mistakes and indiscretions, thus making us vulnerable. Post break-up, how safe will those secrets be? Taking that risk as well as having to start anew can feel rather daunting.

- **'Perhaps I won't find someone else/better/who'll put up with me'**, can sometimes deter us from ending our relationship out of concerns about our future prospects. 'Better the devil I know', can keep us in a relationship which is increasingly a compromise.

And when it's time to move forward

- **When you're sure** that your relationship is definitely over it's important to acknowledge that sometimes we share our lives with others, but maybe only for a limited period of time. Appreciate how the experience has helped you grow into the person you are today. Give thanks for that, whilst also accepting that sometimes we outgrow relationships, as both move on in different directions.

- **Stop and consider** the consequences of staying with someone out of pity, guilt, the fear of causing them distress. How humiliated and disrespected would you feel if you discovered that someone had done that to you? Caring for someone may mean saying, 'I don't love you in the way you deserve to be loved', a painful, but sometimes necessary conversation. It's more humane than staying, and gradually growing to resent and maybe despise them.

- **Falling out of love** yet remaining good friends can happen when open and honest channels of communication have been maintained throughout, especially if children, friends or business interests remain important. Regularly talking things through can ensure that there are no surprises; both know how each other feels, so even difficult decisions can be shared, understood and agreed together. Listening is a key part of this process.

- **Caring for another person** means wanting what's best for them, even if that means breaking-up. It's also about respecting the other person enough to give them the chance to find someone they can ultimately share a loving relationship with.

- **Feeling a failure** can be part of the healing process. Everyone needs time to reflect and grieve after a significant death or ending, and divorce is no different, as it signifies the end of a special relationship and the life we'd anticipated living, possibly after having invested many years into it.

- **During and after our divorce** it's important to take time to process what's happened. Valuable lessons may be learned, regrets worked through, and feelings of failure may need to be healed. Counselling and hypnotherapy can play an important part in the recovery process, by helping with self-esteem, improving the conflicting emotions that may be agonised over (like anger, hurt, frustration, 'why me'), especially if your ex initiated the divorce and appears to be moving on well.

- **It's important to grieve** over what's been said or done, both by yourself and by others. A divorce will have significant impact on virtually every area of your life. It takes time to recover from harsh exchanges of words and actions. You may need a period of reflection to determine your next steps, how to start again, forge a new identity and sort out the practicalities like childcare, financial considerations, work and living arrangements. All these important decisions can reinforce feelings of vulnerability and loss of direction.

- **Children are often a major consideration** throughout a break-up. They may be required to move home or school and may struggle after the trauma of the break-up, no matter how amicably both parents try to handle it. They often need reassurance that they are loved by both parents, that they were in no way responsible for the divorce and can speak to the absentee parent as often as they want or need. Keeping them updated, in an age-appropriate way, can help, perhaps by including them in things like, if a house move is involved, the decoration for their new bedrooms. This enables them to feel more positive, considered and accepting of the changes.

- **Close family** may struggle to accept the break-up and find new arrangements hard to take. But grandparents can be invaluable after a divorce and offer stability and security in a potentially unsettled environment. You often hear that one set of grandparents is relied upon heavily, maybe for housing, financial or childcare support whilst the other side becomes almost estranged. Both sides need to work hard at staying reasonably neutral and avoid too much comment or criticism if they want to retain contact with each other.

- **Home and where to live** is an important decision post-divorce as it has major implications. Separating one home into two is stressful and expensive and can reinforce the sense of overwhelm and failure. Would it be worthwhile to house-share or rent until things settle before embarking on the next big decision?

- **Work often becomes more relevant** post-divorce. There's often pressure to earn money, but this could also be a good time to change career, maybe retrain and use this opportunity to start again. Balancing the desire for a fresh start against the need to earn money can be difficult, but investigate options like night school, working part-time, becoming self-employed and also being prepared to accept offers of support. These may be viable ways to start a positive, new life.

- **There's a great deal to think about here**. Sourcing appropriate childcare, accommodating immediate necessities, deciding how next to proceed, whilst potentially losing your usual support network of friends and family can all add to the stress and feelings of overwhelm experienced throughout your divorce. Already in a heightened state, important decisions can add to you feeling increasingly vulnerable at this time.

- **Individual or relationship counselling** can play a valuable role in helping to improve communications and appreciate each other's point of view. Becoming calmer, more confident, taking things less personally, avoiding saying or doing hurtful things by not lashing out if you're feeling upset or wounded are important things to take away from your break-up.

Negative patterns and reactions need healing in order to avoid repeating similar patterns in the future. Relationship counselling can also help facilitate the process of breaking-up, especially when children are involved. Remember, you loved each other once. Try to take things at your own pace and remember, there's no lonelier place than in a loveless relationship. Your decision to divorce can be the start of a positive new life.

When it's clear that it's the right time to break up

- **Take the bull by the horns** and say that you need to have a chat about your relationship. Over time there will have been subtle changes to your body language and demeanour as you've gradually moved away from the relationship. Be clear that you've something serious to say, so giving your partner time to mentally prepare.

- **Be discreet, respectful**. Yes, you may have discussed your misgivings about the relationship with close friends or confidantes, but if you're the initiator of the break-up avoid the temptation to tell too many others first. It's hurtful and embarrassing if your partner's the last person to discover the relationship's over.

- **Keep the conversation on track** and avoid listing every failure and shortcoming. Be firm and clear about your intention to break-up. Stay on point, that it's no longer working for you. If your paths are likely to continue to cross it's good to remain reasonably amicable, even if you can't remain friends. Aim to end it, rather than let it drag on indefinitely, hoping that they'll end it first; much better than you becoming increasingly unhappy, sour and full of recriminations.

- **Accept that there's a need to grieve**, sometimes before the relationship officially ends, even if it's you who initiated the break-up. It's sad to lose a close relationship and all its future promise. Grieve too for the hurt that's been experienced, the things that you regret, that may be forgiven but not forgotten.

- **Grief can include several stages**; denial, bargaining and negotiation, anger, depression until there's finally acceptance. All can be drifted in and out of. Accept those phases, but sometimes accept too if a good friend says it's time to move on and stop with the analysis and introspection!

Ending the relationship sooner rather than allowing it die slowly can sometimes mean it's easier to keep the friendship or at least some mutual respect.

Find ways to support yourself throughout your divorce

People who've been living in a loveless or disapproving, highly critical relationship for a long time may well experience a significant impact on their mental wellbeing. Depression, low mood, sleeplessness, poor self-confidence and self-belief are not uncommon at this time.

- **Share how you're feeling** with a trusted friend or confidante. It's good to have an ally who's there to offer support and reassurance. Alternatively, your GP or spiritual adviser may be a valuable source of assistance. Or booking time with a therapist could be a positive way to unravel some of the negativity that's built up during the deterioration of your relationship and divorce.

- **Accept that your ex-partner now feels differently** about you and the relationship, an opinion that's been shaped over time, encompassing many different experiences. Their opinion of you is simply their perspective. It doesn't define who you are. You've both changed and grown apart throughout your relationship, fundamentally leading to your divorce.

- **It's often necessary to make quick decisions** around a divorce, in particular concerning living arrangements, schooling and earning money. Try to avoid major, hasty choices that have long-lasting implications and instead maybe look to house share with a friend, so aiming to keep things as familiar as possible at first. Allow some time to grieve, recover and reflect on what you'd like to do next, maybe start by considering the benefit of working part-time.

- **Formulate ideas and plans** for a positive future, no matter how far ahead that may seem. Yes, money could be tight, children often require your full attention, but try to schedule some time for yourself, perhaps to go for a walk, read a book, phone a friend for a chat, enrol for an online course, or even dip your toe into the world of dating.

- **Be proactive**. You may have lost your old circle of friends for a variety of reasons, so start building a new group, one more suited to your present set of circumstances. Other parents, neighbours, work colleagues, even online forums and social media may offer support, companionship and help to boost your mood. Discovering that you're not alone, that others have had similar feelings and experiences from which they've recovered can offer invaluable comfort and reassurance.

As you move into this next stage of your life agree to be gentle with yourself, but also be receptive to new ideas and things you may have never considered before. Open your mind to the possibilities of your new life post-divorce. You're not just moving forward, you're starting anew.

What to tell the children about your divorce?

When a couple are breaking-up it can be difficult to decide what to tell the children. One party may want to reconcile, the other may be clear that the relationship is well and truly over. There's often guilt about getting divorced. The distress can make the aggrieved party want to lash out and hurt the other. Involving the children can seem to be an effective way to achieve that result.

But there are several ways to achieve a beneficial long-term solution, one that helps both children and parents reach a healthy and sustainable post-divorce outcome and positive quality of life.

- **Tell the children about the divorce together**. It's best if you both meet and agree in advance what the children need to know. Accept that you don't love each other in the same way, but still love your children. You're not going to continue living together, but your children can see and/or speak to the absentee parent as often as they want or need. Children want to know the practicalities: how the change will affect them, where they will live and with whom, where they will go to school. They rarely need to know more than how it directly affects them.

- **Financial arrangements** after the divorce can result in one parent having significantly less money than the other. Luxuries and treats may have to go. Children are wise and will happily take gifts of expensive holidays, trainers, mobile phones and computer games off an indulgent parent. They also know their other parent is covering the day-to-day expenses, the food, school uniform, travel expenses and things that remain largely unnoticed. Being unable to afford lavish treats can make the main parent feel inadequate and unable to compete. Agreeing finances so they fairly cover the children's daily expenses can provide a more even arrangement for both parents.

- **Discipline can be a minefield**. One parent may have the children living mostly with them. The parent with less frequent access often wants to ensure the children have fun during their time together, but this can mean that they return home unsettled and unmanageable, sometimes for days afterwards. Consistency about bedtime, sugary treats, television and computer access can provide a more balanced situation for all.

- **Criticising your ex can be tempting.** Sharing details of their unacceptable behaviour throughout the relationship can seem irresistible, especially if the children are behaving badly and causing distress as they enthuse about the lovely time they've had with your ex. It's important to fight the impulse to be negative and accept that children can be manipulative at times. But they know what's really going on and don't need you to vent your frustrations. And at the end of the day your experience of their parent is different to theirs.

Children often see far more than they're given credit for. They know how much effort the main caregiver makes to look after them well, they understand the struggles involved. They're aware when their affection is being bought out of guilt. Supporting children and protecting them from many of the distressing details will enable them to move on with their lives in the most positive way.

Tips to Help Children Cope With Divorce

Divorce may result in children feeling pressured to take sides, to decide who's the 'good' or the 'bad' parent. They may feel they can only be loyal to one, which may mean rejecting or disapproving of the other.

Here are some tips to help children cope with the divorce of their parents

- **An ally is important**. Someone to talk to, whether it be a grandparent, schoolteacher, family friend. Someone who's sympathetic and listens can help a child come to terms with their new situation. A child may initially feel embarrassed or ashamed about their change in circumstances, especially if it means moving home, explaining why one parent is absent or their financial circumstances are very different. They need to feel certain that their confidante is trustworthy, honest, impartial and will not betray their secrets, unless they have no choice and it's essential to do so.

- **Knowing their parents are remaining civil** helps children cope better. Many children fear that they're being disloyal to one parent if they're nice to the other. Seeing their parents communicate and be respectful helps children feel more comfortable and secure throughout the divorce. Children take their lead from their parents. Treating each other with respect and good manners teaches children about adult relationships and positive ways to handle conflict.

- **Remaining calm about one's ex** reassures children, who don't need to be drawn into their parent's dramas. Feeling under pressure to take sides, express negative opinions, be interrogated by one parent about the other are all unacceptable situations for a child. No one wants children to have divided loyalties or feel bitter and angry at the situation.

- **Routine is important to children**. Children cope better when they understand how the divorce will affect their life. Where they will live, arrangements for school, ongoing contact with each parent are all issues of immense importance to a child. They need reassurance as to how they will be affected and questions need to be answered as honestly as possible.

- **Children are adept at playing one parent against the other**. They quickly become skilled at manipulating their parents into getting what they want. After a divorce this situation can be exacerbated by several factors, ongoing tension between the couple, disparity of financial income, the different lifestyles lived by each parent.

These factors can result in one parent feeling that they're perceived as inferior to the other, which may be sensed by their children. In an ideal world each parent should respect their ex's role. The reality is often very different. Refusing to participate in one-upmanship can help both children and the situation settle down.

- **Guilt** is often a serious factor in a divorce. Parents may feel bad about the failure of the marriage, the breakup of the home, disrupting their children's lives. Accepting that their parents are upset about the divorce, even unwell for a time, can help children grieve in their own way. Being able to discuss the new situation helps children talk openly about their feelings, come to terms with them and learn that they don't have to be strong and hide their distress at what's happened.

Reassure children

They are not to blame for their parents' divorce. Both parents still love them. They can contact either parent whenever they want, even by phone or internet. In terms of their routine in the future, what changes can they expect. They can ask questions, which will be answered as truthfully as possible. Their parents divorced each other, not them. Those relationships are a completely separate matter.

TAKEAWAYS

- Your wellbeing has to be a priority so that you can move on well
- When things go wrong it's an opportunity to grow
- Other people's priorities and perspectives may be very different to yours
- Not all relationships stay with us for life
- We're divorcing each other, not the children

66

We spend so much time

analysing differences,

why can't we

concentrate

on similarities?

99

2

CONFLICT AND FAMILY MEDIATION

Mediation cannot change the past, but it can help to shape the future for your family unit in a more positive way.

Conflict in relationships

Conflict exists in all relationships, whether it is a romantic one or between family and friends. Conflict is all around us. It is neither positive nor negative, but a natural force that is necessary for growth and change in life. Sustained unresolved conflict can however create tension within a family unit. If partners are constantly at odds with each other and virtually any situation leads to an argument or disagreement, the marriage might have quite a few unresolved issues. When arguing is excessive, especially if these arguments never result in solved problems, the evidence may suggest that the relationship will not last.

The subject of conflict is deep and detailed and outside the scope of this handbook, but what does matter is how we manage conflict. If it is used constructively instead of destructively, it can lead to positive and purposeful communication, which can in turn lead to positive changes all around us, permeating to our children and wider family. Conflict in the area of divorce and separation, if dealt with in the correct way will have a positive impact on the future family unit.

The parties can move on to the next stage of their lives much more easily when past conflicts have been resolved. Further, when there are children, conflict resolved by way of mediation can help parents to continue to work together for their children, providing for their emotional well-being into adulthood and beyond.

Conflict at the end of a marriage

Ending a marriage or a long-term relationship brings many adjustments, and former partners can find themselves in the middle of confusing and overwhelming conflict. When children are involved, finding ways to manage and keep conflict to a minimum is essential. Whether their parents are married, separating, divorcing or divorced, children react negatively to poorly managed conflict.

Research has documented the impact of parental conflict on children. Children experience stress when one parent hurts the other emotionally or physically. Children are also stressed by unresolved struggles, the use of silent treatment in the home and worries about where they will live.

Although it is never the intention of parents to hurt their children, putting them in the middle of conflict is particularly detrimental to them. Examples of this are asking children to carry messages back and forth, telling children the other parent does not love them, telling children they will have no home to live in or money, and putting the other parent down.

Parents want the best for their children. However, experiencing a high conflict environment can overshadow this desire and detract upon parents acting in the best way for their children's future well-being, both emotionally and financially.

How can mediation help to break the spiral of conflict?

Mediation, although not really understood by many, dates to ancient Greece where village elders used to mediate local disputes between the villagers. It has been around as a method of dealing with disputes for more than 3,000 years.

Today, mediation is a professional service offered by trained, professional mediators. The term mediation broadly refers to any instance in which a third party can help couples to discuss difficult topics, to behave non-defensively which helps reach a long-term, lasting agreement.

In the UK, family mediation has seen a rise as a service since the Children and Families Act 2014 made it compulsory for separating couples to go through a mediation assessment before they could apply to court for a divorce. This indicates to the court that mediation has at the very least, been considered as an option. This is because the option of court does not always bring out the best in couples, can be expensive, long-winded and imposes a decision upon you. Going to court, often referred to as "litigation" tends to focus on past wrongs and grievances, whereas mediation focusses mainly on the present and the future. When you must continue to parent together if you have children and manage the finances for your family, the option of working at it together through mediation is a much more positive option.

Family mediation encourages co-operation and supportive relationships between separated couples and children, but it is not always suitable. Before embarking on the court route, people do need to understand the options of mediation so that they can make an informed decision as to which route they wish to take.

The word mediation is in everyday use, but in relation to family matters, it is still liable to be misunderstood and many still think of it as an attempt at reconciliation or even "meditation" which it certainly isn't! Mediation is an option only when a couple feel like they have come to the end of the road and are ready to sort out the issues of separating or divorcing in the most amicable and dignified way possible. They themselves are coming up with proposals, with the help of the mediator that will work for their family unit.

Mediators themselves see the main aim of mediation as empowering separating and divorcing couples to reach agreement without recourse to court. When you separate there may be so many things to think about it can feel overwhelming.

The worries that many couple say keep them up at night include:

- children, where and who they will live with,
- how often they will spend time with both parents,
- holiday arrangements,
- Christmas and/or other religious events,
- how to financially look after children,
- cost of extra- curricular activities/holidays/education
- the house and whether it will be sold or retained whilst the kids are still young, or should one party buy the other out
- alternative accommodation needs
- ongoing finances,
- pensions, and
- even the family pets

The list and the worries are real and immediate and need to be sorted out to help everyone to move on in the best possible way.

Family mediation is used primarily by separating and divorcing couples to settle arrangements for children and/or financial and property matters. It can also be used to help wider kinds of family matters. Grandparents seeking contact with grandchildren in family conflict or following the death of a parent may need mediation.

In this handbook we are concentrating on divorcing or separating couples, whether from marriage or a civil partnership, and most family mediations in this respect involve the two parties attending the mediation.

Understanding the core principles of mediation before progressing

The guide to Family Mediation in England and Wales, explains four core principles and it is important that anybody thinking about mediation understands these fully:

Mediation is voluntary: Nobody can force you to go through mediation. Even if you do start the process, you can withdraw at any time. It is important to realize that parties are themselves in charge of the process and if it is not working, they do not have to continue. This means that everyone involved can feel confident that they are taking part on their own terms.

Mediation is confidential: it is entirely confidential unless there is evidence of children being at risk, domestic violence or criminal behaviour. Everything that is discussed is shared between the parties but is not valid in a courtroom without the express consent of both parties. This is known as the term "without privilege".

The idea behind this is that mediation very much stands alone and is nothing to do with the court. By attending mediation, the aim is to try and keep out of the court arena.

Mediators are impartial: On so many occasions one or other client will often say at the beginning of the process, "Are you linked to such and such a solicitor?" Or, "Do you know my ex or any of his/her friends?"

The answer is a definitive NO! The mediator is entirely impartial and is acting on behalf of both parties to find an acceptable way forward for everyone involved in the process. Unlike solicitors, family mediators do not act on behalf of one party. They simply facilitate negotiation towards settlement and have no vested interest in the outcome. Mediators must decline to mediate if they have prior knowledge or experience of advising or working with either or both parties in another role or capacity or if they know of either party personally.

Decisions are in the hands of the parties: Mediators help parties to reach their own, well-informed decisions and arrangements. Only jointly agreed decisions will be progressed, and the mediator has no part in that decision-making process, other than to ensure that both parties understand what it is they are agreeing. Mediators can give legal information and guide as to what would seem fair and correct if the matter was to go to court, but they cannot give advice.

Some mediators will come from a legal background, and this may be helpful in navigating the legal issues of a divorce or separation, whilst others may come from a more therapeutic background which will help to guide in matters concerning children.

It is important to remember that as the parties to the mediation you have control in the mediator you choose, how quickly you progress matters, the financial decisions you reach, and the present and future arrangements for your children. Once you go down the court route, all these choices will be taken away from you. Sometimes that is inevitable, as mediation is just not suitable, but you need to make the right choice in such an important decision in your life and take time to think about the options available. That is why legally, before even making an application to court, you now need to attend a mediation information assessment meeting. This will allow you time to consider your options fully and will be discussed in the next chapter.

TAKEAWAYS

Mediation

- seeks mutual interests and common ground
- narrows differences
- helps to build bridges
- aims to reduce conflict and stress
- focusses on present and future arrangements
- helps parties talk and listen to each other

You will not get everything you want, there is no winner in these situations: it is about compromise, negotiation and putting your feelings aside to try and work out a way to get on with your lives.

3

GETTING STARTED WITH MEDIATION

Choosing the Right Mediator

Now that you have decided to proceed with mediation as a possible option you need to look at getting the most out of the process.

Firstly, use your gut feeling and ask yourself if you think you can work with any given mediator. Like any business relationship, personal qualities will play a big part.

Whilst anyone can perform the job of a third party, acting as a mediator, particularly for a couple who are potentially considering divorce, is a specialist area. You only have one chance to get it right and so the right help is vital. It is therefore sensible to choose a mediator who is registered with The Family Mediation Council, which is the leading mediation body, and ensure that those listed are properly trained, supervised and subject to professional standards.

You can check out local mediators on their website, www.familymediationcouncil.org.uk

A registered family mediator may be either accredited or working towards accreditation. All registered mediators will have had previous experience in a professional role. To become an accredited mediator, the family mediator must have submitted a portfolio of evidence of their competence. The standards required for this are exceptionally high and it can take up to three years or longer to qualify on an accredited basis. You may want to check if your mediator is accredited or working towards it. If your mediator is accredited, you will know that they will have had experience and many successful outcomes. You might also wish to ask them about their success rate.

If they are accredited, then you also know they have attained a certain recognizable professional standard and that they are subject to re-accreditation every three years to keep the mediator on their toes. When accredited, all mediators must still undergo regular supervision with a Professional Practice Consultant, and they must continue to attend training courses in both legal and therapeutic areas throughout their mediation lifetime.

Never be afraid to ask your potential mediator about their full credentials. Check whether your mediator is accredited for both children and finance matters via their web site. It is important to feel totally confident in your mediator, and if you do not, then you are totally within your rights to look for another one.

Another important question is the costs of the process, both the initial mediation assessment and any subsequent mediation. The complexity and the range of issues you want to mediate upon will have a bearing on the number of sessions you will need. It is worth bearing in mind that mediation is almost certain to be considerably less expensive than pursuing matters through an acrimonious Family Court route.

The MIAM (Mediation Information Assessment Meeting)

This is the first meeting you will have with the mediator either because you need to make an application to court (you cannot make an application to court without attending a MIAM), or because you want to try mediation to stay out of the court arena, or sometimes even a combination of both.

There are rare exemptions when you do not need to attend a MIAM:

- in cases of domestic violence which have been reported and prosecuted
- threats of the removal of a child from the country
- involvement of social services due to urgency of matter.

Apart from the above, the MIAM marks the first stage of your journey with your mediator, and if you really do want to avoid the court process, you should try to get the best from your MIAM appointment.

Before the meeting have a good think about what you want to say to the mediator and jot down any questions you want to ask. This is your time to talk confidentially about exactly where you are up to, and for you and the mediator to assess whether mediation is the correct option for you. Remember mediation is always voluntary. You cannot be forced to proceed with this process, nor will you be criticised by the court if you decide after the MIAM that it is not for you.

The mediator will talk to both you and your partner/spouse separately, either in person or remotely. It is an opportunity to ask all the questions you want about the process and your understanding of it and to build a rapport with your mediator.

It is important that you feel confident that your mediator will keep you safe and comfortable in the mediation meeting. If you do not feel that you could be in the same room as your ex-partner, be clear about that. It may be that your mediator could consider a different model of mediation, known as shuttle mediation, which will be explored further in the next section.

THE MEDIATION MEETING: How and where will it take place?

Face to face in the office

This is where you both attend in the office and meet with the mediator in person. There will be three people in the mediation, both parties and the mediator. Each session is usually around an hour and half.

Remote Mediation

This is the process of conducting a mediation session via video call/Zoom/Skype. All parties including the mediator communicate remotely which allows for complete accessibility to mediation for anyone at any time. There are strict rules which indicate that there must be no recordings of sessions and that only the two parties and the mediator are in the room, unless there are exceptions allowing a third party and this has been previously discussed. The parties will sign an agreement to mediate to acknowledge their acceptance of this.

Remote mediation has become a very convenient and effective way to conduct mediations due to the Covid pandemic and looks set continue due to the many benefits which clients are extolling:

- It can help greatly for individuals operating on tight time and financial schedules as it requires no additional travel time or expense.

- People suffering from anxiety may prefer the comfort of their own home, or simply those not wanting to have to see their ex-partner in the waiting room or office.

- If people are not geographically near to one another

- The sensitivity of the matter, it may help just not to see one another if there have been issues of physical or mental abuse.

Shuttle Mediation

This is where the two parties in the dispute are placed in different rooms and the mediator moves between them to try to help them reach an agreement. It can be used where the couple just cannot be in the same room as each other or where one or both feel so intimidated by the other, that mediation is unlikely to be successful if they are together.

Some mediators dislike shuttle mediation as it involves a lot of running between offices and having to relay information from one person to another. Others see it as a beneficial way to keep clients out of the court system and to help them reach an agreement, where mediation might not otherwise take place. Most mediators understand that mediating through a face-to-face forum is the best way to resolve matters, but shuttle mediation can really help people who just cannot or should not be in the same room together. And remember if you do go to court, you will have to be in the same room as one another, so it is always a model that should be discussed and considered at the MIAM stage.

For shuttle mediation, you can also bring someone to support you to the mediation which is not normally allowed in face-to-face mediation unless there are exceptional circumstances.

This kind of mediation does take more time (usually two hours) as the mediator will have to move between both parties and disclose all information between the two. It is important to check that your mediator is skilled in this kind of mediation and is comfortable about doing it, and what the cost will be.

Remote Shuttle Mediation

This can be done on-line though a video conferencing platform. This allows both parties to be online in separate rooms. You do not have to see each other on screen or communicate with one another. As with remote mediation, it may have many advantages as worrying about bumping into your ex in the office building or car park can be stressful.

Making the Most of the Mediation Meeting

Once you have decided that you want to go ahead with mediation, you have chosen your mediator and where and how you will have the meeting, it is vital to get your head in the correct place. You need to have the right attitude and an open frame of mind. If you are intractable and unwilling to come to mediation with integrity and good will and an element of compromise, you will not make progress.

You both need to understand that you will not get everything you want; there is no winner in these situations. It is about compromise, negotiation and putting your feelings aside to try and work out a way forward so you can both get on with your lives. Most couples find it is much easier to move forward if they have reached a compromise agreement rather than have a potentially unwelcome solution imposed on them by court. If your mindset is future-focussed for yourself and any children involved, then mediation can really work. Also, it can be resolved as quickly as you both want without having to wait for months, as it would through the court system.

Think About the Issues You Want to Mediate

Consider all the areas that you need to cover. These may be varied (many were mentioned in the previous chapter). The mediator will ask you both what your priorities are. Usually, children and finances are the main focus but it is usually better to stick to one aspect initially and then to move on. The children will always be emotional and conflictual, so it is probably best not to mix the most important beings in your life with the finances. Just take one element at a time.

Remember there is no pressure to reach agreement after the first session. You will usually receive a draft summary a few days after the session detailing what you discussed at the mediation. Then in your own time and, if necessary, with input from your solicitor and or financial/pension adviser, you will have the opportunity to go through everything before any subsequent mediations. Further chapters in this handbook will deal with other professional advisers and the work they do in more detail.

What Happens After Mediation?

So, you have looked at different outcomes and options and have reached a set of proposals that you both think you can live with. How then does the mediated agreement become legally binding?

Your mediator should have explained at the initial stage that reaching an agreement in mediation does not mean that it is legally binding. You and your partner will now have the option of taking legal advice on the outcome. Some parties will have been represented throughout the mediation process. At each stage they will have taken advice from their own solicitor, whereas others will prefer to reach agreement and then take it to a solicitor to check over for them at the end. Although a mediator cannot advise and can only give legal information, by the time a set of proposals is reached, the mediator will be able to say whether it is within the ambit of what is fair for both. Many aspects which may cause concern to a solicitor will have been sorted out.

At the end of the mediation process, the mediator will produce two documents. One is called an Open Financial Statement; this will set out the parties' finances. If the case is child related only, then there will no Financial Statement. The second document is a Memorandum of Understanding. This sets out a narrative of the proposals made by the parties to each other and the outcome that has been reached. This document will set out an explanation to the solicitor as to why the parties have reached their agreement, giving some background.

These two documents should then be passed to your solicitors, and they will then be converted into what is known as a legally binding "consent order" as part of the divorce proceedings. It is important that even if you have not needed the services of a solicitor up until this point, you do now need to engage a solicitor to check over your agreement. It is only at the Decree Nisi stage (known as Conditional Decree of Divorce from April 2022) of the divorce that everything agreed at mediation can be put into the consent order. It is therefore important to know exactly where you are up to in the divorce proceedings when you commence the mediation process, as for most divorcing parties, it is important to know that the agreement can become legally binding and that, once finalised, matters are then closed.

In relation to the children matters, the court does not make an order unless the parties ask it to. There is no court order for child arrangements following divorce. The "no order principle" under the Children Act prevails as it is strongly upheld that what is right for a child at a certain age will change according to their needs. So, an order will only be made if proceedings have already started or there is some particular reason why an order is needed. That is why the courts so strongly encourage mediation in child matters.

After a child-related mediation, the arrangements for the child can be set out in a mediation child summary prepared by the mediator or in a parenting plan.

Child-Inclusive Mediation

An increasing number of mediators are trained and qualified to talk directly with children and young people whose parents have chosen to mediate and who consent to their children being spoken to by a mediator.

This can often be a helpful way for parents to understand how their children view matters and what is important to them. This is not a way for children to make their own decisions, but just for their voice to be heard, which is so vital when parents are separating.

Usually, mediators will only invite children who are ten years old or over and it is the child's decision whether they decide to come and talk with them.

Not all mediators are trained to carry out this work so make sure you check this with your mediator if the option becomes relevant. If a mediator is qualified to see children, this information will be available on the FMC Register: www.familymediationcouncil.org.uk/find-local-mediator

If My Mediation Agreement is Not Binding, Will it be a Waste of Time?

Most parties who have put hard work and effort into mediation and many hours of emotional grit will honour their agreement. All the research that has been carried out indicates that when parties have reached a conclusion themselves, the decisions are more likely to last. Without doubt, the process can be emotionally draining, but because the parties have taken ownership of the decision-making process in a way that is not possible through the more adversarial court route, they generally honour it. This is because they have worked it out together with consent.

Always bear in mind that mediation is a more holistic, versatile and creative route to resolving issues. The door to mediation always remains open. Sometimes, even if matters have been successfully concluded, there may be issues which need to be re-addressed months or years later, such as arrangements for children (which will always vary according to their needs), maintenance variations or the economic climate.

Maintaining a good relationship with your mediation service is important if you need further sessions or clarification. So many people who ended up going through the court system have said they wished that they had given mediation more of a chance because going through court felt like they had lost their control. Most family mediators can give couples a real insight into what the court process is like. As soon as the court application is received, the court takes over and the couple's control to make the most important decisions is diminished.

Mediation can, with the right support, help separating or divorcing parties achieve a fair financial settlement and a happy life for their children.

TAKEAWAYS

- Explore all available options
- Legal costs may be avoided or greatly reduced
- Agreements can be reached quickly
- Consensual decisions are more likely to last
- Parties discuss issues on their own terms
- Mediation can be informal, private and flexible

If given the choice, in my experience, couples still want to be able to talk to each other after the dust has settled, most particularly if they have children together. So, the process of sorting everything out, and their experience on that journey is so important.

4

ALTERNATIVE DISPUTE RESOLUTION – DIVORCING WITHOUT COURT

There Are Other Options to Court

For many years I have been helping families deal with the fallout of separation. The one pervasive thread is that it is never easy. Alongside the disentanglement of the family finances, is the unravelling of what can be decades of emotional attachment, resentment, baggage, whatever you want to call it. But the two exercises can rarely be undertaken in isolation, very few of us can remove the memories that were created in that house, or the intentions that were set down for that investment when the account was opened, and the blood sweat and tears that went into accruing it.

Now traditionally when couples separate, if disputes arise about finances, the court has been the default route to a resolution. But I invite you to just sit back in your chair for a second... What images does the word "court" throw up for you?

Animosity perchance?

Fighting?

One-upmanship?

The desire to win?

Judge Judy/Rinder?......I jest; but the common perception of a court is that it is a battle, not only between the couple, but the lawyers, with all the ensuing bitterness and unfortunately, the costs that follow.

Invariably, if given the choice, couples still want to be able to talk to each other after the dust has settled, most particularly if they have children together. So, the process of sorting everything out, and their experience on that journey, is so important to give them a fighting chance of being able to pick themselves back up, dust themselves off and get on with the daily practical issues of co-parenting, or just moving forward productively into the next chapter of their story.

So, if Not Court, What Else?

These days there is a plethora of options out there available to the separating couple. ANY of these can be used. Believe it or not YOU are in charge of how you conduct your divorce or separation. However, in order to do that, you should make sure that you are as informed as possible about all of the options.

Part of your journey is to find a lawyer whose practice suits YOU and how YOU want to deal with your separation. Some lawyers have a reputation for specialising in non-confrontational ways of resolving disputes, some a reputation for heavily contested High Court battles. You must find a lawyer that is right for YOU. If that means shopping around a bit, then you absolutely should do that. Don't forget the average separation will take between nine and twelve months to finalise, even if things are really amicable, and so you and your lawyer are going to go through the metaphorical mill together. Make sure you choose the right one to make that journey with.

Any lawyer you go to see should talk you through the alternative dispute resolution options open to you....and yes, the meat of this chapter is to briefly walk you through those choices.

Mediation

Covered in the previous two chapters in detail, but I will say that this is the absolute mainstay of alternative dispute resolution (ADR), as you might hear it being called. All cases these days have to show that they have at least attempted mediation before a court application can be made.

If a case fails at mediation or it is a case not suitable for mediation (because of violence in the relationship or something of the like) then the mediator produces something called a MIAM certificate so that an application can be made to the court. But the salient point here is that this method is open to absolutely everyone. It is usually conducted by a third-party independent mediator, who can help guide a couple to a resolution. They can't advise though...bear that in mind, so after mediation you would generally go back to a lawyer for some advice on the prospective deal, and then the final consent papers would be drawn up.

It can be a very quick and efficient way of boxing things off. Sometimes though, if a couple's finances are a bit more complex and trickier, or there is mistrust about one party being untruthful about disclosing all of their assets, then mediation can sometimes be a damp squib and something a little "stronger" is needed.

However, in all my years of practice, I find this method to always be my first port of call for couples. In a great many cases, early intervention by a mediator can prevent things turning sour for you before you get anywhere near real animosity.

Collaborative Law

In the family law legal world, this can only be described as the "Marmite" method of resolving matrimonial disputes. In some parts of the country, it is incredibly popular. That is because in those areas, bands of lawyers who subscribe to this method have formed productive and sensible groups that promote this way of working. In other areas of the country, it is not very popular at all, mostly, in my view, because the practitioners in that area are not fans. So, whether or not this becomes an option for you will probably largely depend on the lawyers you instruct and their location.

It is largely an American concept that for these purposes has been anglicised. It involves both parties at the beginning of the dispute instructing lawyers that are trained in this practice. Both parties then sign up to an agreement that effectively says that they are wholly committed to this process. If for whatever reason communication breaks down and a court application becomes the only option, they will then agree to instruct fresh lawyers to take things forward. This "pact" in many ways focusses the minds of couples committed to this way of working to reach a resolution. For that reason, amongst many others, when both parties and the lawyers are committed to this process, it can be an absolute winner.

The process consists of a number of "four-way" meetings. Initially, the couple and their respective lawyers commit to a number of meetings, where an agenda of what will be discussed and covered in each meeting is agreed. Also, outside experts can be brought into the discussions, like a financial adviser, a mortgage adviser, an accountant, divorce coach or counsel (otherwise known as a barrister), if necessary. Basically, whatever the couple want and need to bring a resolution in to focus.

When done well, this process can be fantastic. It doesn't though necessarily mean that it is quicker or cheaper than any other method, but it can be fully bespoke and for that reason some couples have sworn by it.

Arbitration

Now in legal circles, arbitration has been around for a very long time. It is an established method of dispute resolution. But in the family law world, it is a fairly new phenomenon. At the start of a dispute, the parties can decide together, through their lawyers invariably, that they are going to opt out of the court process and agree to arbitrate.

This is a process where the couple choose their representation, choose their judge and choose the venue in which they want any hearings to be dealt with. Nowadays, and of course post-pandemic, a lot of this (as can all methods of ADR) can be conducted via a digital platform of choice. The embracing of technology in the legal world has undoubtedly sought to speed things up and keep costs down. Whilst we are still learning in this arena, the benefits have been undeniable.

Once a couple agree to arbitrate, they can choose to conduct it in a quasi-court fashion, that is with a directions hearing, a dispute resolution hearing and a trial, or if they are part way there with their discussions and just need a sticking point of law to be unlocked, so that they can get over that and finish their settlement, arbitration can be used for those discrete points. If it is used like that, it is popular for an arbitrator to simply receive the papers from both sets of lawyers and for a decision to be given in writing.

When parties decide to arbitrate, they agree and acknowledge that they will be bound by the decision. The huge benefit of arbitration is that the timetable is decided on by the couple, not an over-burdened and under-funded court service.

The arbitration judge when dealing with the case will probably only have that one matter that day and can properly prepare, instead of a judge in the court service who will maybe have five or six hearings that day and limited time to get to grips with the papers. All in all, arbitration is an excellent alternative to court proceedings. In theory, the cost of using this method is probably similar to court proceedings, as generally the process will look very similar.

The major plus point though is that there will be no delay and the couple is in control of the timetable for the most part. It is becoming more and more popular with separating couples, but still not a mainstay of the average divorcing family. It is much more popular in big money cases. However, there is no reason why this method cannot be accessed by everyone, and with post-pandemic backlogs in the court, this might become an established alternative to courts up and down the land.

Private FDRs

FDR stands for "Financial Dispute Resolution hearing". It is normally the second hearing that happens when parties use the court process to deal with their financial dispute. Couples can now use private FDR's to try and help them reach a conclusion. These are very popular in big money cases and for those who can afford to conduct them.

Generally, these come about when proceedings have been issued at court, the first directions hearing has happened, but the court-lead FDR is going to be many, many months ahead, and the parties just want to move forward. Much like arbitration, the couple, through their lawyers, can choose a judge, a venue, a timetable and so on.

The big difference is that the couple is not bound by the "indication", or suggested financial settlement decision, the private FDR judge gives them. So, if they don't agree with what he or she says they can put the matter back into the court system and can either opt for another court-lead FDR with a different judge, or they can go straight to a trial.

An FDR is a hearing where the judge has looked through all of the papers and has heard the arguments from both sides. The judge can then decide, if they were going to make a judgement at a trial what order would they make. They take that view and give an "indication" to help the couple and their lawyers go outside and use the day to try and negotiate a settlement.

I have attended private FDRs where the judge has then used the rest of their time after giving an indication, going between the two parties' rooms and doing their best to help them with any issues they are struggling with.

Most couples who choose to use this route, because they have paid extra to have this alongside a court-lead process, use this time to agree a settlement.

Round Table Meetings

I have to say this is one of my absolute favourite ways of finding solutions for couples. Again, it can be a really quick and pragmatic way of coming to a resolution.

Generally, this is a meeting that is set up once disclosure has been exchanged between lawyers, any questions have been asked and replied to, and valuations of assets have been obtained, and where the couple can't reach an agreement themselves. There is then nothing to stop the parties' respective lawyers setting up a meeting, with one party in one room, the other in another room and a middle meeting room for the lawyers to negotiate.

This is traditionally how a round table meeting is set up, so the parties (contrary to the label) don't have to sit across from each other awkwardly at a table, whilst their lawyers argue it out. Parties can all sit round the table if they want to, but most people prefer to set it up as I have explained. Here there is no judge, or independent tribunal. This is all about the parties doing their best to pragmatically reach a settlement that works for them both and their family.

Between Yourselves!

Oh yes and lastly, before I forget, there is always your kitchen table! Never forget that this is your separation, your family, your divorce. If circumstances allow and it feels right for both of you, once you have taken legal advice (or not if you prefer not to), some of the most sensible deals can be done round the kitchen table, between the two of you.

A word of advice though, if you do manage to resolve things this way, always make sure you formalize your agreement into a consent order that is approved by the court, but if that's the only bit you need a lawyer for, you've done very well!

TAKEAWAYS

Never forget that YOU can take charge of how this is conducted. There are choices; you don't have to immediately go to court.

- Choose your lawyer wisely, they will be with you for the long haul. Make sure that you research their practice, and you are happy that they will act in line with your values.

- Consider all the options for alternative ways of resolving your dispute and if one fits make sure that you get thorough advice about how that will work for you and your case.

- Remember not all options will be right for every case and the unique personalities involved.

> *If you weren't the one who looked after the money, you might be feeling totally overwhelmed now that you have to look after everything yourself.*

5

HOW TO UNSCRAMBLE YOUR FINANCES

Overwhelmed by Finances

Most couples operate as a team. Each person looks after the areas they are best at. Maybe one of you looks after the house and the other looks after the garden, one does the DIY and the other the car mechanics, one looks after shopping and the other takes care of the finances and bills.

If this has been the case in your household, and you weren't the one who looked after the money, you might be feeling totally overwhelmed now that you have to look after everything yourself. The thought of getting your head around detailing your expenditure, collecting your financial information together and negotiating your financial settlement is terrifying you. Even if you have previously looked after the money, the need to understand the finances to the degree necessary to reach a fair financial settlement can be tricky.

In this section, I will help you to understand some of the financial basics you will need in order to take the next step forward.

Marital Assets

You will hear phrases such as "Marital Assets" or "Matrimonial Assets" referred to by lawyers. What they mean are the savings, investments, pensions, property and other valuable things acquired during the course of the marriage, including inheritances received during the course of the marriage, even if only by one spouse. Non marital assets refers to the personal property acquired before the marriage or after you were separated. However, this does not **guarantee** that they will be ring-fenced out of being divided in the divorce.

Financial information – what do you need?

Whether you use a mediator or enlist the help of a solicitor, before you can agree how to divide your finances between you, you will need to provide financial information, which is called financial disclosure. This may be completed and exchanged with your ex through solicitors using a Form E or at the point of applying for the financial consent order, using the D81 form. These forms can be found on the www.gov.uk website. We will also include links to them on our own website.

You will need to gather information about **all** your assets (for example, house, savings, pensions, investments), liabilities (such as mortgages, loans, credit cards), income and expenditure. You will need to declare everything, even if you believe some of your assets are non-marital and should be ignored.

Assets

Valuations of each of your assets are essential to get a full picture of everything that you own as a couple, both individually and jointly. The valuation figure will need to be accompanied by supporting evidence, such as a statement or a professional report.

For some assets, the valuations will be straightforward, for example, the value in a bank account is the balance, which is confirmed by the bank statement. However, for some you may need to enlist professional help.

You should get any residential property valued, preferably by three different estate agents, and commercial property by a commercial agent. Business valuations should be requested from an accountant, preferably someone independent. For pensions, you will need to request the CETV (Cash Equivalent Transfer Value. More on this later) from your pension providers, along with details of the benefits provided by those pensions. Let them know it is for divorce purposes, so that they include the costs associated, which you will need during the negotiation stage. You should also get an indicative value of your vehicles using an online valuation site.

A general list of the documents that will be required for the Form E is on our website, www.yourdivorcehandbook.co.uk.

Pensions

The complexities around pensions mean that they deserve a section to themselves. There are two broad types of pensions: defined benefit and defined contribution. Let's start by looking at each type:

Defined Benefit

When you have a Defined Benefit Pension, your retirement pension will be related to the salary that you earned whilst working in the job which it relates to. You will earn a proportion of your salary for each year you work. For example, for an 80th scheme, if you worked for 40 years in a final salary defined benefit scheme where your final salary was £80,000, you would receive 40/80 of £80,000, which is £40,000. These schemes are now commonly moving to Career Average, rather than Final Salary, where the payments are linked to the average amount you earned during your employment, rather than your final salary.

You will need to request a CETV from the scheme provider, letting them know it is for divorce, which will be free of charge as long as you haven't already requested this within the last twelve months. This will be calculated by the scheme actuary according to the scheme rules. However, it may not represent the value of the benefits being provided by the scheme, so allowing you to compare the benefits available from different schemes. More on this later.

Defined Contribution

A defined contribution pension may be related to a job, such as a Workplace Pension or Group Personal Pension, or may be a personal arrangement, such as a SIPP or personal pension. Rather than having a known benefit at the end, within these pensions you build up a pot of money, which can be used on retirement to provide you with income in the form of an annuity (guaranteed income for life), income drawdown (flexible withdrawals, which are usually drawn to meet your needs) or a combination of the two.

Again, you will need to request a CETV from the scheme provider. Usually this will be the same as the value of the pot. It is worth mentioning that if the pension has any guarantees, such as Guaranteed Annuity Rates or Guaranteed Minimum Pension, the CETV may again not represent the value of the benefits.

It's My Pension

Pensions cannot be in joint names. Therefore, many people believe that they should be able to keep their own pensions when they divorce. This is not necessarily the case. As with a lot of areas of divorce, it depends on your circumstances, but it is important to investigate any pensions to ensure that you are not just giving away valuable assets. Pensions are often the second biggest, and sometimes the biggest, asset after the house and should go into the pot of "marital assets", along with the house, savings and investments.

State Pension

On top of the other pension benefits that you may have, it is important to include your state pension benefits. You can request these from www.gov.uk/check-state-pension. You also need to check that your National Insurance record is correct as, whilst it is unusual, mistakes can be made. There are circumstances under which the state pension can be shared. They can also make a significant difference to the income you receive in retirement.

Actuarial Reports

If there are a combination of defined benefit (DB) and defined contribution (DC) pensions, or if there are DC schemes with guarantees and without, or different DB schemes (for example, NHS and Barclays), you should request an actuarial report. The pension actuary will help by valuing the pensions in terms of the benefits to ensure they are comparable. They can also calculate what equalising income at retirement age looks like, what equalising the capital values looks like and how the value of the pensions could be offset for other assets.

An actuary is generally instructed by each of the couple's solicitors as a Single Joint Expert. They can be instructed directly but you may wish to take advice on the information you would like in the report to ensure you ask for the right things. There is a sample letter in the Pension Advisory Group's Guide to the Treatment of Pensions on Divorce and more information on using a Pensions on Divorce Expert (PODE) in Advice Now's *A Survival Guide to Pensions on Divorce*. Both of these documents can be found online or links to them on our website.

Liabilities

As with assets, you need to detail your liabilities. For any credit cards, you can simply provide the latest statements, which usually arrive monthly, or can be downloaded. However, for mortgages and loans, you will need to request a "redemption statement" from the lender (phoning them is generally quickest). These can take a few weeks to arrive, but they are necessary to see the actual amount it would cost to repay the mortgage or loan in full.

Income

If you are employed, payslips and P60s can confirm your income. If you are self-employed, you should provide three years' self-assessments. Directors of limited companies should provide three years' accounts for the business(es). You may have a number of different income streams. You should gather information about all of them. You should also provide twelve months bank statements from all accounts.

Expenditure

It is this section of the financial disclosure that many people find difficult. There is a budget planner on our website www.yourdivorcehandbook.co.uk which you can use to assist. You should complete this in terms of current and also what your future expenditure, is likely to be once you are divorced or your civil partnership is dissolved.

Start with the basics. These are the rent or mortgage, gas, electric, water, council tax, food and transport for you and your children (if you have them) when they are with you. Don't forget that you will receive 25% discount on your council tax if you are the only adult in your property.

You can then start thinking about other essentials, such as TV licences, debt and/or loan repayments, clothing, footwear, uniform, house maintenance, car servicing and so on.

Finally, you should add in lifestyle discretionary expenditure. This is probably the most difficult section to complete. You will want to maintain your lifestyle as far as possible. However, if money has been tight in one household and between you there are now two households to support, it may not be possible to live exactly as you did previously. However, for the purpose of providing the information at this stage, you should disclose the costs of continuing to maintain your lifestyle.

It is important to try to be as accurate as possible with your expenditure. So, try to think of everything you spend money on. This should include gifts, entertainment, holidays, subscriptions, gym membership and other lifestyle costs. You should also think of the miscellaneous purchases that might be a book one month, pair of earphones the next and laundry basket the month after.

You also need to detail any capital purchases you will need to make. For example, if you are the one who has moved out, you may need to purchase new furniture, crockery and suchlike. It is important to include these one-off expenditure items.

What Do You Need?

The information we have talked about gathering together in this chapter, will be used to understand your needs in terms of income and capital. With some divorces, there are significant assets over and above what both parties need. However, we will be discussing only the case where the assets just meet, or don't meet, the capital and income requirements of both people.

Income Needs

To work this out, we need to look at the budgets created for the Form E. If the required income (expenditure, including pension contributions for your future) for both parties exceeds the income being generated, there will need to be some compromise and restrictive belt-tightening.

You should already know the level of income that you receive now. There may be some other income that you could receive or be entitled to:

- Child Benefit – If your spouse has been a higher earner (over £60,000 per annum), they will either have had the child benefit reclaimed through their tax code or may have opted not to receive it at all. However, once you separate, you may be able to claim it again. It is worth checking whether you are entitled.

- Child Maintenance – This depends on the amount of time that your children spend with each of you. If the share of the children is 50:50, no child maintenance needs to be paid. If not, the person who has the children with them for less nights will then pay child maintenance to the other. You can use the Child Maintenance Calculator at www.gov.uk/calculate-child-maintenance to work out the basic figure but you may want to look at this figure in respect of the lifestyle your children have been used to, as it is really only inclusive of housing, food and clothing, not extra-curricular activities. The child maintenance agreed by couples is often higher than this figure. Also, it is sometimes paid by the higher earner, even if the caring of the children is 50:50.

- Spousal Maintenance – If you have taken time away from work to bring up children, taken a step back from your career to support your spouse or will need to increase your earnings by returning to work or working full time instead of part time, you may be in a position to ask for payment of spousal maintenance. Recently, it has become more common for this to be payable for a short-term fixed number of years, rather than for life. This enables the lower paid spouse to secure a new job, get some training and suchlike. For a clean break, it may be possible to "capitalise" this amount, which means receiving a lump sum to replace the regular income. As a couple, you will need to have sufficient assets to do this, such as investments and savings.

- Universal Credit – If you are going to be on a low income and have limited capital, you may be entitled to claim universal credit. You can see how much you might be entitled to using the link www.gov.uk/universal-credit. It is important to note that this will be reduced by maintenance payments.

- Earned Income – As we discussed earlier, you may be in a position where you need to earn more. If you work part time, you could see whether you could increase your working hours. You could begin a "side hustle" (a business that you run in your spare time in addition to your full time job), apply for a promotion, apply for a new position elsewhere or retrain to a job that pays more. We cover these in more detail in Chapter 11. Whilst these options may take time, you may be in receipt of spousal maintenance in the short-term to cover the difference.

You will need to understand what level of child maintenance and spousal maintenance you need to receive or are able to pay so that when you negotiate with your spouse, you are able to enter the negotiations from a place of knowledge.

Capital Needs

When we look at capital needs, we are looking at sharing the assets of the marriage. However, it is worth considering what share of the assets you need. You need to consider the following:

- Housing – this is considered the most important by the courts. We will discuss this area further in chapter 7.

- Transport – will you need to buy or lease a car, or do you have to replace one you have in the very near future?

- Furniture and home equipment – If you are moving out, you may need to buy items for your new home.

- Pension – we covered this earlier in the chapter, but it is important to understand the retirement income you will need, how the pension benefits you have will meet this and the share of your pensions that you might have to pay to your spouse or be in receipt of.

If the needs of both parties outweigh the marital assets alone, non-marital assets, (that is, those accrued before or after the marriage) may be brought into the mix.

Testing a Settlement

Whether you are using mediation, collaborative law or family lawyers to negotiate your settlement, you are likely to receive from, or make an offer to, your ex. However, do you fully understand what this offer means to you in the context of your life and lifestyle? Will you be able to maintain your lifestyle? Will you need to earn more and if so, how much? These and many other questions relating to the offer can be difficult to answer. Working with a divorce specialist financial planner can help you to see how the settlement offer might work for you and your family.

The financial planner can collect the Form E information, along with the offer being made, and will use special software to produce a model showing what your life will look like if you accept the offer being made, or if you make the offer you wish to. You may be able to see that a tweak to the structure of the offer, for example, a larger amount initially in exchange for a smaller pension share might leave no shortfalls.

The same software can also be used to test the lump sum realistically required in order to have a clean break, which is where you would pay or receive a lump sum, instead of ongoing maintenance, which can be preferable if there is sufficient money available.

Understanding the position that you will be in financially after divorce is vital to help you to move forward, giving you clarity and peace of mind for the future.

TAKEAWAYS

- Get a complete picture of ALL the marital assets
- Understand what your lifestyle costs now and in the future
- Don't ignore the pensions, they're valuable assets
- Work out your needs, income and capital
- Understand that compromise will be needed.

You need legal advice. You need to know what you are financially entitled to, and you need to know what will happen in respect of children arrangements.

6

HELP, I NEED TO SEE A SOLICITOR

What do I do?

So, all the attempts to either work out a way forward for your relationship through counselling, or the attempts to try to work out separating or resolving finances or arrangements for the children by one-to-one chats or through mediation have not worked.

You need legal advice. You need to know what you are financially entitled to, and you need to know what will happen in respect of arrangements for your children. Or maybe you have taken advice before you embark upon discussions or mediation.

Whatever route you have taken on this path, how do you find a solicitor? What should you expect? How much will it cost? All these questions are likely to be racing through your mind at this uncertain time.

The first thing to do before you see a solicitor about divorce, dissolution or separation is to **BE PREPARED.** The more information you have when you start to have discussions with a solicitor the better, but don't worry if you feel that you don't have the information available to you.

Try to obtain information and make a list of all your joint and individual assets which include:

- Property

- Pensions

- Investments

- Income

- Bank accounts

- Trust funds

- Business management accounts.

- Overseas investments

- Inheritance

- Anything that might be financially relevant.

Try to find out valuations of properties, mortgage redemption statement(s), transfer values of pension funds, values of investments, details of all bank accounts, details of all business management accounts, how much you both earn. Everything.

Even if a relationship post-separation seems to be good, and let us hope it stays that way, often when you start to discuss money, it can bring out the worst in people. You are no longer your spouse's priority and he or she may be feeling the need to protect all their financial interests. They may be reluctant to share so, as a starting point, please be prepared and have as much information as you possibly can for your first meeting with a solicitor.

How do you find a solicitor?

Ask around. Look around. Like any service that you might be looking for, you want the best quality at the best value for money. What is your budget? Remembering that, often with the large plush city centre practises, that is what you are paying for – plush offices.

Maybe browse the internet. Have a look at websites. You should ask friends and family for recommendations, after all if you needed a builder or plumber or any other service, you would probably go on recommendation.

Do shop around. Some solicitors will offer a first meeting for free. You need to think whether you will be able to work with this solicitor. It is about building a relationship over what can be nine to twelve months. Maybe longer, but hopefully not. You need to feel comfortable. You need to feel that they understand you and your situation. Do not always assume the more expensive is better. Sometimes you can really pay over the odds for mediocrity.

Your first meeting - what to expect

It is likely in your first meeting that your solicitor will ask you lots of questions to find out about your situation. If you are upset or tearful that is fine. You will not be the first and they should put you at ease. It really is a meeting to get to grips with your situation and what help you need.

They will probably start by asking you some basic questions, such as your date of birth, date of marriage and then more probing questions about where your relationship is up to. Is there a way forward? If you are thinking of divorce or dissolution of civil partnership, they should follow with questions about property, outstanding mortgages, savings, pension funds, income. Everything financial, which was covered in detail in the last chapter.

All the time your solicitor will be processing your information and thinking about the divorce/dissolution law and how to apply it to your case.

Once they have taken down all your information, they will move onto.......

Advice: Divorce

This is where the solicitor advising you will start discussing firstly, the grounds for divorce. The law is changing on the 6th of April 2022 and will completely alter the present five factors that need to be chosen and will be moving to a no-fault divorce (More on that later).

But at present, to obtain a decree of divorce you must firstly have been married for a year and you have to show the court that your marriage has broken down irretrievably evidenced by any one of the five following factors:

1. Adultery (but not for same sex marriage or same sex civil partnership)
2. Unreasonable behaviour
3. Two-years separation with consent
4. Desertion (very rarely used)
5. Five years separation without consent.

In each case the procedure is the same. The petition is prepared and is sent to the court with the fee of £550 to be issued and posted out to the other party. They have to return an acknowledgment form indicating they have received the papers.

If your spouse does not return their acknowledgment form, if you have based your petition upon unreasonable behaviour or five years separation, then you can arrange for court bailiffs or a private process server to personally serve, (that is hand) the divorce papers to your spouse.

You are a bit stuck if your petition is adultery because there has to be an admission of adultery, so do think before you issue an adultery petition if you think your spouse will not admit adultery as this is a requirement. Also, if you have issued a two-year separation petition, you are also a bit stuck as the ground requires consent of the other party.

If you have anything in writing from your spouse, such as an email or text saying that they have received an unreasonable behaviour or a five-year separation petition you can look at what is called deemed service, where the court will accept that your spouse has received the petition. If all else fails, the court can dispense with service of the divorce petition but you have to show that you have exhausted all avenues to bring the petition to your spouse's attention.

Once they have either returned their acknowledgment form or you have other evidence either personal service or deemed service then the petitioner can apply for decree nisi. Decree nisi is the approval stage where you ask the court to approve your divorce petition. Six weeks and one day after decree nisi you can apply for decree absolute which will finally dissolve your marriage.

It all takes about six months, sometimes longer. If there are finances to resolve your solicitor might advise waiting until there is agreement or court order in respect of your finances before finally dissolving your marriage.

Very rarely nowadays is a divorce contested as the courts take the view that when one party has decided they want a divorce then there is no point holding the marriage together.

The law is changing on the 6th of April 2022 so that the either or both parties can file, with the court, a notice stating that the marriage has broken down, obtain a conditional order and, after six months, a final order for divorce.

The new law will be to file the application for a divorce order, wait 20 weeks before we can apply for the conditional order and then a further six weeks before we apply for the final divorce order.

It has removed the need to set out any fault in terms of adultery or unreasonable behaviour and the timescale will be the same as previously, five to six months.

The change in the divorce law in April 2022 is a positive change for an outdated and acrimonious fault-based system which has been welcomed by lawyers and separating couples alike.

Your solicitor will then likely move onto...

Advice: Finances/Money

As previously explained, the Form E is a document that is completed both where voluntary disclosure is being given and also within court proceedings. A solicitor will advise you that the first step to open up discussions is for you both to provide voluntary disclosure usually in the format of a Form E, which is a very detailed document which both parties individually complete. The information required is detailed in Chapter 5.

Your solicitor will want a full picture of both your respective financial positions. Lawyers use the phrase "the matrimonial pot." You will hear that discussed a lot. The idea being that you both get all of your assets - capital, income and pension fund, and put them into an imaginary pot, then divide them up fairly in accordance with a list of factors called the Section 25 factors (more on that later) with the first consideration being given to ensure any children of the family have a home.

So basically, put all your assets into this imaginary pot and then divide, although not necessarily 50/50. The divorce courts have a wide discretion to do whatever they think is fair.

You might hear or read horror stories from friends or read horror stories on the Internet, but please remember everyone's case is different. Everyone's case is fact specific so what applies in your case might not apply to someone else.

If you have children, things will be approached slightly differently, as the children, and the need to provide a home for them, is the court's priority, as is how the parent with whom they do not live is going to support them financially.

Always remember the three things: income, capital and pension fund. That is, how are you going to live day to day, where are you going to live and how are you going to fund that plus any additional capital, is there pension fund to provide for your future? Always have those thoughts in your mind and keep an eye on the long-term outcome.

After your solicitor has taken details, he or she will want to look at the mutual exchange of financial documents. Nowadays, this involves the completion of the Form E, mentioned above.

As discussed in chapter 5 this sets out income, capital and pension fund together with monies received and outgoings per month. The idea being that once you have full disclosure you can then start discussing proposals for settlement.

If agreement cannot be reached, then the Form E is updated and used in a court process.

What am I going to get? How will I live? Where will I live?

All these questions will be going through your mind. You will want your solicitor to advise you and whilst they cannot give guarantees, you will want advice as to the range of outcomes.

As was mentioned previously, the family financial courts have a wide discretion.

Every case is fact specific, and the court will look at every case as unique, applying a list of factors called the Section 25 Matrimonial Causes Act 1973 factors.

These state that the welfare of any minor is the first consideration and the need to provide a home for the children. Then consider:

a) the income, earning capacity, property and other financial resources which each of you has or is likely to have in the foreseeable future, including in the case of earning capacity, any increase in that capacity which it would in the opinion of the court be reasonable to expect a party to the marriage to take steps to acquire

b) the financial needs, obligations and responsibilities which each of you has or is likely to have in the foreseeable future

c) the standard of living enjoyed by the family before the breakdown of the marriage

d) your ages and the duration of your marriage

e) any physical or mental disability of either of you

f) the contributions which each of you has made or is likely, in the foreseeable future, to make to the welfare of the family, including any contribution by looking after the home or caring for the family

g) the conduct of each you particularly if that conduct is such that it would in the opinion of the court be inequitable to disregard it.

In essence, all assets will need to be valued and so, you may have to employ surveyors to value properties, accountants to value businesses or actuaries to report on pension funds.

The idea is that you are both open and honest. Sometimes that does not happen but that in itself would be a full chapter!

All you need to know for the basics is that the court want to know everything. You and your solicitor are entitled to know everything.

You may be fortunate to have agreed everything with your spouse or partner and that is to be applauded. Your solicitor will still want to run through all the details to check it is a fair settlement and even if there is a financial agreement on a divorce or dissolution. This will need to be set out in a consent order which is sealed and approved by the court.

How should you feel after your first meeting with the solicitor? What do you take away from that meeting? Next steps?

So that is roughly what your first meeting with a solicitor should involve. There will be a lot of information to digest and take in. Ideally, your solicitor should follow up with a confirming email. You should leave that meeting feeling reassured.

The divorce or separation may not be something you would have chosen, or you may be the one seeking separation, but you should have an idea of the grounds for divorce on which to use if you are going down that route, how your finances are likely to be approached and arrangements for the children.

You may need to discuss arrangements for your children which your solicitor will discuss with you in your first meeting. These are dealt with later in Chapter 8.

Your solicitor will have explained all this to you, and you should feel confident that you are in safe hands.

Moving on from the first meeting. We have completed and exchanged Form E - what now?

This is the time to consider with your solicitor - do you have all the information you require? Has your spouse provided everything?

It is generally hoped and anticipated that you both will provide full disclosure but if not, your solicitor should explore with you what is not right, what is missing, what does not make sense. A detailed questionnaire can be prepared asking about anything that does not make sense and which needs clarification.

You can only start negotiating once you have a complete picture of what is in your "matrimonial pot" that is: what assets are on the table for discussion.

If information is not promptly forthcoming, then you should look at making an application to the court within a reasonable time frame. Don't hang around. If it looks as if things are not moving along or information is not being provided, then get an application to sort out finances (Form A) sent to your nearest Family Court.

Please remember, once you send an application in a First Directions Appointment (FDA) which is a timetabling hearing but it is not listed for a hearing until after three months. The idea being that within those three months you both prepare Forms E (which you are likely to have started in voluntary disclosure) so those would just need to be updated.

Negotiating - how it's done

If you have all the information you need, your solicitor will start discussing what your needs are for capital income and pension fund in light of your available assets. Your solicitor will always have the Section 25 MCA 1973 in their minds applying them to your case.

Remember those factors which are stated above.

Remember, too, the priority is to make sure children, if you have them, have a home. Every case is fact specific. You may not like the advice you receive. It may not be what you want, or think is fair, but be open-minded, as the courts have a very wide discretion to do what they think is fair and reasonable with any financial assets.

If your case is complex, your solicitor may suggest a conference meeting with an experienced family barrister. Often other input can be invaluable. Sometimes three heads really are better than two. Be open-minded about cost – sometimes you have to invest to make sure that you get a good, fair and proper outcome. Also, be open-minded as to what is suggested and discussed. Ask questions of your solicitor and barrister if you use one.

How do the Section 25 factors apply to your case? It may not be as straight forward as a 50/50 share. But always bear in mind – income, capital and pension fund; that is: somewhere to live, investments for the future, if possible, income to live day today and pension or investments for the future.

As mentioned in Chapter 5, offers that you make or are made to you can be tested by a financial planner, so that you understand what they mean in the context of your life.

You reach an agreement - what happens?

If you manage to reach an agreement, that is great!

It has to be recorded and set out in a detailed financial consent order that your solicitor will draft and will be signed by you both. This has to be sent to the court and approved by a family judge who, as well as dealing with cases on a day-to-day basis, has paperwork to do and approving or declining consent orders is one of those paperwork tasks.

There is usually no need to attend court if you have a financial consent order, but be aware that it can be declined if the judge thinks it is unfair to one party or that more information is required.

You are required to complete a D81 - Statement of Information. Often this does not provide sufficient details to enable the court to consider if it is a fair settlement so often, we prepare an addendum to the D81 which gives additional information.

In essence, in D81 the court need to know: what are the assets in your case? How have you both agreed to divide income capital and pension fund? Does this provide a home for the children? What are your respective incomes? Is it a fair division, again having regard to all the matrimonial assets and the section 25 MCA 1973 factors as mentioned on page 64?

If the courts are happy with the agreement, then it is sealed by the court and is legally binding upon you both. The practicalities of implementation now happen that is ownership of any properties are transferred, lump sums paid, and pensions shared.

It is always hoped that the terms agreed in a financial consent order can be implemented promptly so that you can both move on with your lives.

We cannot agree on finances - what happens?

If you cannot agree, then an application to the court (Form A) will be sent into the Family Court by your solicitor. There is a court fee of £255. The court then set a First Directions Appointment (FDA) in approximately three months' time.

The court will also set a date for the mutual exchange of the two completed Forms E. A date will also be set for preparation of any questionnaires if after receiving your respective spouses Form E you believe information is missing. In some cases it is necessary to instruct experts, actuaries to comment on pension fund and forensic accountants to comment upon businesses. All this is discussed at the FDA.

The court process is covered in detail in Chapter 9. Do have a look through the court process in case you need to travel down that road. It is always hoped that agreement can be reached but the financial divorce courts are there to help if needed.

TAKEAWAYS

- Look around for a good, competent solicitor

- Go to your meeting with a divorce solicitor prepared with as much information about finances as you can

- Remember the grounds for divorce, that is: irretrievable breakdown evidenced by one of the five factors but also remember that the divorce law is changing in April 2022

- Advice regarding finances: what goes into your "matrimonial pot" and the factors which are applied under the divorce law (S.25 Matrimonial Causes Act 1973) to your case

- Try to agree a settlement after full disclosure of all financial information and ensure that all negotiations ensure a fair outcome

- Make sure any agreement is set out in a financial consent order approved by the court

- If there is no agreement, look at getting an application sent to the court to resolve finances as it could be many months before a hearing date is listed.

> *The Bank of Henry can only offer Henry Mortgages. It cannot offer George Mortgages offered by The Bank of George down the road, even if George Mortgages are offering a better deal.*

7

MORTGAGES

Let's Start at the Beginning

Finances are a huge consideration when contemplating divorce: do I need to work, can I afford to stay where I am, what will my lifestyle look like? These are just a few of the many stressful questions that can plague us during this unsettled time.

There are many factors to consider. Our living arrangements are often at the top of the list, even more so if children must be considered. It's not only about what you can afford. If you have children for example, parental access is important, as is the continuity of their education. Then, what about family, friends, work, lifestyle and the quality of where you live? So, if you need to buy a new home, you may need a mortgage.

Discussing your situation with a mortgage adviser can give you helpful and unbiased information as to your position, what you can afford and the different options available to you. This support can help you to feel more confident about these important next steps and help you avoid some expensive mistakes. But when is the right time to start speaking about mortgages? As early as you can is the answer. It is potentially a very confusing time and a mortgage may seem like the least of your worries. Having the insight, however, into what your future borrowing capacity looks like is key for so many reasons: from initial settlement negotiations to simply easing your own anxiety of knowing that you can and will have a roof over your head in your new life.

Guess Who?

Not all mortgage advisers are the same. Have you banked with the same bank for decades and think they will therefore be as loyal to you as you have been to them? I would suggest you think twice. Making sure you see an independent mortgage adviser is pivotal to ensuring you receive the right advice, not just getting access to the cheapest products on the market. It is not always just about price. Did you know you not all mortgage advisers are the same?

How are you supposed to know the difference I hear you ask - well, as a rule of thumb, those that work in a bank, can only offer you their own products, that is, The Bank of Henry can only offer Henry Mortgages. It cannot offer George Mortgages offered by The Bank of George down the road, even if George Mortgages are offering a better deal.

Then you have those that work in an estate agent. These are often (but not always), 'restricted' which means they will have access to a number of lenders such as Henry Mortgages, George Mortgages, Lucy Mortgages and Elizabeth Mortgages. If they are restricted, they don't have access to ALL mortgages.

Lastly, you have advisers that work for a mortgage brokerage. Usually, you will find that these are available to offer mortgages from 'whole of market' which means they have access to all the banks, building societies and other lenders that don't fall into either category but still offer mortgages.

With regard to those that offer advice and those that don't offer advice - this can vary between all three. Before engaging in any full conversation with you, an adviser must share and go through their 'Initial Disclosure Document' (sometimes referred to as Terms of Business). This is a standardised document which will confirm to you upfront, before starting any form of appointment, either face to face or on the telephone whether: 1) they offer products from a single lender, restricted number of lenders or they are whole or market and: 2) whether they offer advice or give information only. It is a regulatory requirement for this to be shared before any conversation starts in detail so make sure you insist on it so you can choose for yourself whether to proceed any further knowing what you now know.

Why a Mortgage Broker?

Along with confirming the scope of service, the initial disclosure document will also confirm how the adviser is remunerated. Differences include commission from the mortgage lender, a fee charged by the adviser or a mixture of both. A common question is, "Why should I pay for a broker when I could go to the bank direct?" There are lots of answers to this but let me explain just five.

Firstly, brokers regularly have exclusive rates available from the banks and building societies that are cheaper than the actual lender offers themselves.

Secondly, your broker has expertise, knowledge and experience to not only find you the cheapest mortgage, but the most suitable mortgage. There are literally thousands of mortgage products on the market each week.

Thirdly, your sanity. A small forest is killed when a mortgage application goes through. We do not want to add any additional stress, pressure or paperwork to an already full desk at this time in your life. Your broker is going to deal with everything for you, with you only being required to provide information they don't have.

Fourthly, their experience of problem-solving helps them to think outside the box. Not every lender assesses every application the same. Where one lender may say no, another will say yes. Where one may offer you a mortgage of £100k, another may offer £200k.

Lastly, support and a friendly face when you need it. Does your bank adviser work at 9pm on a Tuesday? Can you WhatsApp them on a Sunday? If something goes wrong, how quickly can you get hold of them? Do they have administrator or PA support? I guess the answer is "No" to all of them.

First Things First…

So, it is now the time to get the mortgage - but what is the actual process? How does it all work? What if I haven't ever dealt with a mortgage before? It can be very daunting, money certainly is.

First things first - you need to find your adviser, and you need to be comfortable with them. You need to trust them. You need to be able to be honest and open with them. You need to understand what they can offer you and be 100% happy they are working for you, not just themselves. Your adviser will get to know all about you, your name, address, income, shoe size, blood type (only kidding), and you will get to know them. It is as much two ways as it should be one way. As part of this, you will both be able to explore your options and funnel down what it is you are able to achieve. You can ask as many questions as you want and hopefully you should leave the meeting with a clear idea of what your new home life could look like!

After that meeting, you will more than likely have agreed for your adviser to organise an initial 'Agreement in Principle'. This is a certificate that shows after some initial checks (credit check, document checks and affordability), that all the information you provided, has shown that, in principle, a lender will lend to you what has been discussed. This is where it gets more exciting, it starts to feel more real. You will need this if you want to view any properties. Estate agents usually insist on it to make sure you are in a financial position to proceed. (Don't let them force you to see their own mortgage adviser for 'financial qualification'. You can tell them you have your own and show this to prove so!). Your solicitor might also want a copy to prove you are able to proceed with a mortgage of some sort.

It's Mortgage Time!

Then it's mortgage application time. This comes when you either: 1) find a house and have an offer agreed or 2) are ready to re-mortgage your property to complete a Transfer of Equity (remove your ex from the mortgage on your family home) and/or release equity (borrow extra so your ex can buy whilst remaining on the mortgage for the family home). It is at this point you agree the nitty gritty of the mortgage itself such as rate, cost and suchlike before you sign your life away!

Affordability

Getting a divorce is going to throw all your finances into the air. There can be a change of income and outgoings galore. This can be further heightened if children are involved. You may need to start work, increase or decrease your working hours, start receiving benefits or maintenance or be committed to paying maintenance - a whole host of different circumstances can be created as a result of a divorce.

In terms of how you are assessed by a mortgage lender, employed people and self-employed people are treated differently. Put simply, employed persons are looked at in terms of what they are expected to earn going forward, that is: what does their remuneration package state they will earn in the future, their salary. A self-employed person is generally looked at in terms of what they have already earnt in the past, which is a big difference. That said, it isn't always the case; some lenders will take projections for self-employed persons and some lenders want history for an employed person's variable income, such as bonus and commission. Again, this is where having a good, quality, independent mortgage adviser is paramount, as they will know what lenders will and won't lend to you based on your individual circumstances. Do not listen to your friends in the pub, and do not get lost in *Google* thinking all lenders don't lend to people who have just started a new job or have only been self-employed for one year - it isn't true!

Income

Nearly every type of income will be taken into account by one lender or another. Not every lender, however, takes into account every type of income. All lenders have different appetites for risk and therefore will accept different income types, whether this be guaranteed or not. Not all types need to have had history. The types of income to remember to declare are maintenance, benefits (including child benefit), new jobs, self-employment (including second jobs), commission, bonuses and overtime.

Liabilities

As with income, all lenders treat all liabilities differently. Whether this be credit cards, loans, other mortgages, pension contributions, maintenance, or childcare. Some may take a percentage of an outstanding balance or consider the monthly payment as a commitment. It can be the case that there are already set calculations for affordability for every borrower regardless of their own liabilities, or weird and wonderful formulae used based on number of children and suchlike to determine affordability. Again, every lender works differently, some ignoring commitments, some weighing more heavily than others.

What Can I Borrow?

This question is as easy as, "How long is a piece of string?" There is no magic equation. It isn't as simple as a multiplication of income, as it may have been in the past. It may sound like a broken record, but again every lender calculates every borrower's lending capacity differently. Where one lender may lend you £100k, another may lend you £200k as already mentioned. It can really be as different as that. Ensure you see an independent mortgage broker who will assess your circumstances and match you with the best lender for your needs. If you do this early on in the process, you will have a clearer picture from day one about your options.

Lastly, you will need to review your protection requirements such as life insurance, critical illness cover and income protection. Any prior insurance policies you may have had with your estranged partner may become void. Of course, your circumstances will be changing anyhow so this is the time you will review your needs as there will be lots of things to consider now you are parting ways. Your adviser will go through your different options with you.

It is advisable to update your will at this point too, as divorce revokes, or annuls, any previous will. It is also worth noting that, should you have the good fortune to win the lottery whilst separated, (and not yet divorced) but the bad fortune to die before you have made a new will, your estranged partner could be entitled to your winnings.

Mortgages are a complex world. That's what keeps mortgage advisers in a job, just like your solicitor, mediator, financial planner or counsellor. Seeking professional advice in all aspects will reap dividends for the next chapter in your life.

TAKEAWAYS

- Check that your mortgage adviser can give advice and look for it to be whole of market

- Know the details of all your income sources

- Let the adviser know ALL your liabilities

- Ask for an Agreement in Principle (sometimes called a Decision in Principle)

- See a mortgage adviser EARLY so that you know what you can borrow!

> *The Family Courts take the view that, as parents, you are the best people to work out arrangements for your children.*

8

CHILDREN

Child Arrangements: What happens to your child/children? How do you sort out arrangements?

Ideally, you should look to sort out arrangements for your child/children by agreement. The Family Courts take the view that as parents, you are the best people to work out arrangements for your children. They will only get involved if they have to. The Family Courts also work on the basis that it is best for the children of parents who are divorcing or separating to maintain an ongoing relationship with BOTH parents.

You may think that your spouse/partner is an absolute moron, that their behaviour towards you is outrageous, hurtful and dreadful but it has to be REALLY bad and usually towards the children before the court will consider stopping children spending time with a parent with whom they do not live.

The Children Act 1989 – which is the relevant law that governs how arrangements for children are dealt with - states that no court shall make an order which will end after the child has reached the age of 16 unless it is satisfied that the circumstances of the case are exceptional.

However, this does not apply to arrangements as to where or with whom a child will live which can continue up until the age of 18. The reality will be that when children reach age 15/16 they have a significant voice as far as the Family Courts are concerned.

Parental Responsibility

The Children Act 1989 also introduced a new concept of "parental responsibility". This is until the child is 18 but again children reaching teenage years are likely to be more vocal in major decisions.

Parental responsibility means the legal rights, duties, powers, responsibilities and authority a parent has for a child and the child's property.

A person who has parental responsibility for a child has the right to make decisions about their care and upbringing. Important decisions in a child's life must be agreed with anyone else who has parental responsibility.

The following are examples of important decisions in a child's life that should have the agreement of everyone with parental responsibility:

- Where a child lives.
- Whether or not a child has medical treatment.
- How and where a child is educated.
- Which, if any, religion a child follows.
- Deciding a child's name and registering their birth.
- Giving consent for a child to leave the country, whether for a holiday or permanently.

The idea is that both parents have an equal say in what happens to their child. Both have equal standing legally. Neither parent is legally more important than the other.

The following have parental responsibility:

- the mother of the child.

- the father of the child providing he is or was married to the child's mother.

- the father of the child, where the child was born after 1 December 2003 and where he is named on the child's birth certificate.

- anyone who is given parental responsibility under a Parental Responsibility Agreement or Parental Responsibility Order.

If you do not fall into those categories, you can obtain a parental responsibility agreement or order. Generally nowadays, both parents tend to have this legal concept.

The law relating to children changed in the 1989 Children Act to move away from ideas of *ownership* of children to be very child focused and it is about meeting the child's needs not either of the adults' needs.

What is best for the children and how are the children's needs met?

Usually, but not always, children will live with their Mum and spend time with their Dad. This is not always the case but often it is Mum who is the primary carer.

Sometimes parents think an arrangement where the children spend equal time between both parents is appropriate. It is whatever works for each individual family, particularly given their children's age and what their needs are.

The starting point is that it is important for the children, their emotional well-being and development to have an ongoing loving and positive relationship with both parents. It is likely that your children will love you both, will be upset that you are separating. Even children whose parents are in a toxic relationship will still feel a loss when their parents separate.

It is anticipated and expected by the Family Court that parents will put their children's needs first. So, if your spouse's parenting is not as good as yours - that they do things differently - if it is good enough parenting, then the Family Court will want relationships to be maintained subject to that being best for the children.

It takes a lot to convince the Family Court that it is not in a child's best interest to have an ongoing relationship with a parent. On separation a child's emotional needs will be for stability, continuity and to be kept out of the adult dispute.

You will have criticisms of your ex-spouse/partner. You are only human, but really do keep your criticisms to yourself. Your kids do not need to know. The Family Court and judges get very cross with parents who put their children in the crossfire. If you are angry, tell a friend or get out the anger in whatever way works for you - just do not share it with your kids. They really do not need to know.

Arrangements

If you can work it out, that is great.

If not, and there is dispute, one of you will need to make an application to the nearest Family Court to where the children reside for a child arrangements order.

There are a range of applications that can be made to a Family Court depending on the nature of the dispute and the law is found in Section 8 of the Children Act 1989.

1. **A Child Arrangements Order** - to determine where children should live or how their time should be spent.

2. **A Prohibited Steps Order** - which prevents one parent acting in a way that the other parent disagrees with, such as changing a child's surname or moving abroad, changing schools or coming

into contact with another person without the other parent's agreement. This is an order to prevent something happening.

3. **A Specific Issue Order** - If a parent wants the court to make an order on a particular issue such as school, religion, medical treatment or living abroad, the court can be asked to determine what is best and make an order. This is an order to give permission for something.

At all stages, the court is child-focused. This law is over 30 years old but is still relevant today and the overriding principle is that *the child's welfare is paramount* and that decisions are made that are in the *child's best interests*. Obviously, you as parents may have different views as to what is in your child's best interests so the Family Court may have to make that decision for you.

The Welfare Checklist – what is this?

The court will make their decision about what orders should be made in your case by having regard to the welfare checklist that is set out in Section 1 (3) of the Children Act 1989.

These are:

1. The ascertainable wishes and feelings of the child concerned.

2. The child's physical emotional and educational needs.

3. The likely effect on the child if circumstances changed as a result of the court's decision.

4. The child's age, sex, background and any other characteristics which will be relevant to the court's decision.

5. Any harm the child has suffered or maybe at risk of suffering.

6. The capability of the child's parents (or any other person the court finds relevant at meeting the child's needs).

7. The powers available to the courts in the given proceedings.

This is the checklist that the Family Court will consider when deciding what is best for your child or children. It may not be what you want or what you think best but it might be what you have to live with.

Practicalities - You need to make an application - What do you do?

Firstly, unless there are issues of domestic violence you need to attend a mediation MIAM meeting with an accredited mediator.

Chapters 2 and 3 have dealt with Mediation. Do have a look through them to see if mediation is appropriate in your case. You then need to prepare a Form C100 and send it to the nearest Family Court to where the children live with the court fee of £215.

The court will then set a First Hearing Dispute Resolution Appointment (FHDRA) usually eight to ten weeks after your application is sent in (depending upon availability). This hearing is just a timetabling hearing and is also to see if any agreement can be reached.

Prior to the FHDRA both of you will be telephoned by CAFCASS (Children and Family Court Advisory and Support Services).

The role of CAFCASS is to provide the court with information and recommendations concerning timetabling or what should happen in your case. CAFCASS will contact you by telephone and will also carry out safe-guarding checks with the Police and the Local Authority to see if either have had any involvement in your family.

They will then send a summary letter into the courts advising of the outcome of those conversations and checks and making recommendations as to what should happen next in your case.

CAFCASS safeguarding must be available at the FHDRA hearing, so make sure that you have spoken to CAFCASS prior to the hearing. At all stages, the court expect attempts to have been made to reach agreement. You are encouraged to try to agree and if you reach an agreement this will be put into a court order.

If there is no agreement at the FHDRA then the court will timetable matters further possibly requesting:

1. Statements from you both.

2. A report from Social Services if involved in your family.

3. A report from CAFCASS if there are welfare issues - these usually take 12-14 weeks.

4. Any drug/alcohol testing if this is an issue.

5. A schedule of allegation (Scott Schedule) if there are issues of domestic abuse or other allegations.

6. Any other assistance the court requires to progress matters such as police disclosure.

Matters are then listed for a further hearing after all the evidence is available.

Sometimes the court will list matter immediately for a final hearing, where the court will hear evidence from you both, but are likely to list for a Dispute Resolution Hearing to see if all evidence has been provided and again, to see if any agreement can be reached.

Your solicitor at both hearings will have discussions with you and your spouse/partner's representative (if they have one) to see if agreement can be reached and to narrow the issues that are in dispute.

If matters progress to a final hearing, then you may have a barrister involved as both of you (and CAFCASS if involved) may have to give evidence to the judge who will ultimately decide.

The court will consider the applications that have been made, apply the welfare checklist and decide, in the absence of agreement, what is best for your children.

Moving on - What happens if I do not think the order is the right one?

At all stages, the court will apply the welfare checklist and often any order made for child arrangements will be a compromise and neither party gets the exact outcome that they want. Any order made will not solve all your problems. No court order can do that. All the court can do is set the basic framework within which you both and the children have to work.

As parents, you both have to have an ongoing relationship for the rest of your lives – easier said than done particularly if your former spouse/ partner shows narcissistic tendencies or sees the children as a way of getting back at you.

Obviously, one of you will be disappointed if the court grants permission for the children to move abroad or change schools, but it may be something you just have to live with. If orders are breached, that is, not complied with, then one party can apply to the court for enforcement.

When considering whether to make an enforcement order, the court must be satisfied that making the order is necessary and proportionate to the seriousness and frequency of the party breaching the order.

The court will consider:

- The reasons for the non-compliance
- The effect of non-compliance on the child concerned
- The welfare checklist
- Moving forward, whether advice from CAFCASS is required
- Whether the parties should attend any dispute resolution programmes

If a court is satisfied beyond reasonable doubt that a person has failed to comply with a Child Arrangement Order, it has the power to enforce it in a number of ways:

- Referring the parties to a separated parents information program (SPIP) or mediation

- Variation of the Child Arrangement Order, which could include a more defined order or reconsideration of where children are living or who they are seeing

- An enforcement order or suspended enforcement order

- An order for compensation for financial loss

- A fine

- Committal to prison

There is an expectation from the Family Court that orders are complied with and it does not take kindly to either party who knowingly breaches a court order. Please do consider whether any non-compliance is about *your* views of your former partner/spouse. As hard as it may be to be objective, the Family Court expects you to be able to put aside your own feelings.

Also, the Family Court will never allow lack of financial support to impact upon a parent seeing a child – this often seems particularly harsh, but the Family Court expect that parents will financially support children or that financial orders are made within a divorce or assessments made by the CMS (Child Maintenance Services).

What you should bear in mind is that the Family Court, when making orders relating to children, are not interested in you or your ex-spouse/partner. The court will listen to what you say but, as harsh as this sounds, do not really care about you or your former partner – they focus on what your child/children need and will only do what they think is best for the children.

So, it is the children's welfare that is paramount in determining what arrangements should be post-separation. This can often be a tricky and fraught area as what each parent wants may be different so do your best to try to reach agreement, but the Family Court is there to help if you are not able to agree or if mediation has not worked.

TAKEAWAYS

- Try to work out arrangements for your child/children by agreement if you possibly can.

- Remember that the court view both parents as having equal legal standing in relation to children and actively want to promote a relationship between children and their parents.

- The child/children's welfare is the most important consideration if the court has to make any decision – this is above anything else.

- If you have to make an application to the court, there are various applications that can be made: Child Arrangements Order, Prohibited Steps Order and Specific Issue Order.

- Do consider the "Welfare Checklist" as this is the checklist that the court will consider when deciding arrangements for your child/children. The court is ONLY concerned with what is best for the children and this may be at odds with what you may think is best.

- Do understand the practicalities and timescales if you make an application and remember that the court expects any orders to be complied with or they will look at enforcement proceedings.

> *There are so many myths that fly around about what going to court is really like, and what it entails. Every case is different, and every litigant will have their own unique experience.*

9

SO WHAT REALLY HAPPENS AT COURT THEN?

The theme of this book for the most part is about avoiding the need to go to court and doing everything you can to try to resolve your dispute in a sensible and pragmatic way. But we all know that sometimes that's just not going to happen. Sometimes, no matter how sensibly you approach the problem, if your ex is entrenched in their view, difficult, not engaging, lying even, then sometimes you will have no option other than to ask a judge to help.

A lot of the time, if a Financial Remedy Application has to be made at court, we still hope that things can be sorted out long before the case gets anywhere near a trial, or a final hearing, whichever term you might want to use. Sometimes, if you have an errant soon to be ex-spouse who is dragging their heels, the timetable that the court affords provides some sensible and authoritative structure to help reach a final deal. So, having to go to court is not always a bad option.

However, there are so many myths that fly around about what going to court is really like, and what it entails. Every case is different, and every litigant will have their own unique experience. So, it doesn't always help to listen to your mate down the local pub. Chances are the facts of their case are wildly different to yours and the representation they had at court was different too.

So, I'll wade through this minefield with some simple terms explained. These are things we as lawyers throw around every day, but if you are new to this stuff, you will need a guide.

Solicitor

Okay this seems like an odd one to start with as the term is so commonly known, but the role is often confused and misunderstood. Solicitors are usually your first port of call in the office. They are the practitioner that will take instructions from you from the beginning and advise you in the round. They will help with the gathering of your financial disclosure, letter writing and processing the case. Some solicitors will also represent you at court if needs be, or conduct round table meetings and the like, as I have explained earlier. But that will depend on the experience, level of skill and competency and general time availability of the solicitor. Most of the time, the solicitor will brief your case out to a barrister if things start to get contested and end up in court/private FDR/Arbitration and suchlike.

Barrister or sometimes referred to as Counsel

This is the one at the bar in court, not in the local coffee shop! These practitioners generally deal with your oral representation at court, in arbitrations, private FDRs and suchlike. In other words, these guys tend to be the ones on their feet talking to the judge or tribunal. As they tend to be in litigated circumstances most days of the week, they have more experience in the cut and thrust of the courtroom, and therefore are better placed to deal with this side of things for you. It would be normal for you to have a meeting with your barrister and your solicitor before any court hearing so that you can agree on strategy and tactics. If funds allow, it is best to have the solicitor also at the hearing with you, to assist you and the barrister, and then after the hearing they know exactly what has taken place so that they can pick up the baton back at the office.

Judge

This is the person that deals with the hearing. Their role is to make sure that the case is being dealt with properly. At a directions hearing, they will give an order to progress the case, like an order to value properties or obtain medical evidence. At an FDR, they will act like a chairman at a meeting and give the parties an idea of how they would see the case settling, and then help the parties and their representatives with any difficult points of law and procedure to begin to reach a settlement. At a final hearing or a trial, they will listen to all the evidence and make a final judgement. The judge is there to help, believe it or not. They want cases to settle, as they see how silly things can get if parties decide to argue about small incidental points that are costing lots of money and depleting the overall matrimonial pot.

Some judges have a reputation for being quite stern and have been known to strike fear into the hearts of barristers and solicitors alike. However, that image that has been made so famous on TV dramas and films doesn't really exist anymore. Judges are there to make sure justice is done, cases are run properly, and parties reach a settlement if they can, before he or she has to make a final decision.

First Directions Appointment (FDA)

This is the very first hearing you will come across if you have to go to court. There is often a big build up to this hearing, as you will have exchanged Forms E beforehand, raised questionnaires of each other and looked at what things need valuing or taking apart. So much work gets done in advance, but when you arrive at the hearing a lot of the time, if your solicitor is on the ball and it's possible, directions can be agreed quite easily, or there may just be a minor argument about a couple of things, such as who or which company is going to value the house. Clients often feel like it is a big anti-climax! No one gives evidence, and it is generally not very exciting. A lot of the time, if it is straightforward, your solicitor will handle it themselves without a barrister. Sometimes it is dealt with on paper without anyone actually attending at court. But do not be fooled by its apparent ease. It is an essential hearing to make sure that all the potential issues are covered so that when we get to the next hearing, we can begin the negotiation process. If you do have to attend one of these hearings in person, it would be incredibly rare that you would have to say anything at all, and the procedure may be completed quite quickly!

Financial Dispute Resolution Hearing (FDR)

This is normally the second hearing that you will attend if you are dealing with your matrimonial finances at court. Usually it is also your last, as most cases settle at this point. It basically is a negotiation day. Ahead of the FDR, both parties will have exchanged offers and drawn their line in the metaphorical sand. The judge will have all the financial information in front of them. However, sometimes because of court time pressures and the current backlogs, they will have had limited time to read them.

A good barrister will have made sure that there is a schedule of assets that everyone can work from, and a full written run down of all the issues and arguments is given to the judge in advance. Usually, both barristers will have done this giving their positions from each respective side. The FDR day usually begins with you meeting with your team and discussing the strategy for the day (which you should have been cobbling together for some time before the actual hearing day). The judge then calls everyone in and, most of the time, listens to the abbreviated arguments from both barristers (as they will have read the submissions). The judge then asks the lawyers any questions they may have for clarification of any facts and suchlike, so that they have a full understanding of all the issues. The judge then gives something called an indication. In other words, if they were the judge at the final hearing and had to make a final order, what would that look like. They usually give an approximate range for the final settlement to lie within, to help the parties then effectively go outside and try and settle the case.

Courts usually afford everyone as much time as they need to do this, as commercially, once you have reached the FDR stage, it is invariably the right time to try and settle a case if you can, as moving onto the next stage will undoubtedly raise your costs considerably.

The parties then retreat back to their respective rooms with their lawyers and mull over the indication that the judge has given. Now, because matrimonial law is so discretionary, you can get ten different judges and get ten different indications, on the same case!! Sometimes an indication can be favourable, sometimes not. If an indication is too unfavourable to one party, that can sometimes cause the other party to dig their heels in on their position and not encourage settlement talks at all, as one party feels more aggrieved than the other in the position they have taken. There is a very fine line that a judge has to tread. If, however, you get a rogue indication that does not assist at all, it sometimes forces parties to take the matter to a trial, but thankfully this is not a regular occurrence.

Once the indication has been dissected by the parties individually, the lawyers then meet, and negotiations begin. A good legal team will have already discussed with you what your settlement parameters are before the hearing, and so will have a tactical plan in place to start negotiations. And so, this is how the day unfolds, back and forth until a deal is struck!

I have to say though, and sometimes this is not the most popular adage to raise with clients, but my old pupil master used to say to me that a good deal is one where both parties feel like they have lost something. What an odd thing to say you might think....isn't this all about winning once you go to court? Well, no. If a compromise is going to be reached on both sides, both parties will have to budge. That is THE only way a deal will be done. Clients who want to stand on principle once we get to this stage, have to have deep pockets, as principles cost money to take matters further! You tend to find that the little issues that were so important at the beginning become less so once you reach this stage. Now, that's not to say that your legal team will not strive to get the best deal possible for you, but in order to draw a line under things at this stage, an intention and mentality of compromise goes a long way to reaching a conclusion.

And lastly here are just a couple of practical tips: don't forget to bring some food and water. You are likely to be stuck in the same room for most of the day. Without something to eat and drink, your energy levels really do drop in the afternoon, and you don't want to be in a position where you are being asked to make decisions about your future without being fully fuelled. Also, try and get as much sleep as you can the night before. Being clear-headed on the day of the FDR is invaluable.

Final Hearing/Trial

Believe it or not, trials rarely take place in the cut and thrust of the family law world. The emphasis is upon settling your case as early as possible. For the most part, the system is set up that way, and trials are there as a last resort if everything else has failed, or if there is a point between the parties that is so entrenched that only a judicial decision will do. The images you see on the TV about court consisting of witnesses trembling in the box, tend to be of criminal trials, not family ones for the most part.

Now, that's not to say that these hearings do not happen, they absolutely do, but everything in our power as lawyers has been done before we reach this stage to avoid it. That's why most settle at the FDR.

To have to go this far, the parties will have spent considerable sums in legal fees, as the burden of preparation and gathering of evidence has grown. The hearings usually take place over a number of days and the costs for attendance of the legal team will have also grown exponentially. The benefit of incurring this cost and the stress of going through a trial has to be commercially worth the risk in my view. A good legal team will have weighed all this up with you in advance.

Some trials, where there are only issues of law, as opposed to issues of fact that are at stake, may be dealt with just by the barristers making their arguments and submissions to a judge before he/she makes their final judgement. But most will need issues of law and fact decided upon. When issues of fact need to be thrashed out like, for example, whether the husband is in fact living with his new girlfriend and that is central to how the finances should be dealt with, oral evidence will need to be heard.

In advance, written statements from the parties and any witnesses will be compiled on whatever issues are in dispute. Mostly these are called narrative statements and cover the parties' views on all the discretionary factors that can affect the case. Sometimes, if there has been a valuation that one party absolutely does not accept, evidence can be introduced to test that valuation, by bringing in a fresh valuer and they both may have to give oral evidence to help the judge decide what they prefer!

At the actual hearing, this is where the husband, wife and other witnesses will get up and give oral evidence. They will also be cross-examined by the opposing barrister. So, when people say they want their day in court, this is it!

Giving oral evidence can be a very stressful time, especially when what you have said is being dissected by the other barrister. Some people relish this experience, as it is their chance to have their say. Others really struggle under the pressure and find it a very difficult experience indeed. That is why taking matters to this degree needs to be thought out very carefully.

The major point to hammer home about a trial situation is that if a hearing runs to conclusion, the court will give a judgement: it will impose an order on the parties. It is then completely taken out of our hands. As I mentioned above about the ten different judges......the same applies here, and unless you can appeal (which is a whole other book!) you and your ex will be stuck with it. I guess what I am trying to get across is that litigation, once you get to this stage, is a real gamble. You should only let matters progress to this stage with strong and solid legal advice and, in my view, if the stakes are high and only an order from a judge will do.

I've written this chapter on the basis of face-to-face hearings. But now post-pandemic, it would be wrong of me not to give a cursory nod to video hearings. When we first went into lockdown in March 2020, the court was very slow to respond. The system was just not set up for volume remote hearings. However, to be fair to HMCTS it has now for the most part got the show on the road.

Many hearings are now done virtually, especially FDAs and FDRs. This is largely because evidence as in a trial is not needed. Parties can enter their own virtual rooms with their legal team, just as they would do if they had their own individual rooms at court.

The positives of them seem to be that court waiting times on the day have now been eliminated. It used to be that even if a hearing was listed at 11am, you might not get on until 2pm for example. But now as all the parties have to dial in at a certain time, efficiency has got much better.

The negatives are that when everyone is at court, especially for an FDR, there is a certain feeling on the day. Everyone has turned up and, most of the time, that impetus is there to settle. I think with remote hearings, the impetus is not quite the same. However, as I said, mostly they are still successful, if prepared well by the legal teams.

Remember though that what I have told you here is a brief canter through the various circumstances that commonly take place when someone goes to court. You will have your OWN unique experience with your OWN case. The best take-away I can give you is that If you are embarking on court proceedings, make sure that you are happy and comfortable with the team around you. They will provide you with advice and support which will make all the difference as you navigate this transformative time.

TAKEAWAYS

- Every case is unique, everyone will have their own experience. Comparing the experience of friends is rarely useful.

- Know your team - who is the solicitor, barrister and judge and what their roles are. It is surprising how much misunderstanding exists here. Knowing this can really help you get to grips with the proceedings.

- Understand the pattern of hearings that is likely to take place, and make sure that your team explains them to you in detail, their purpose and what is likely to happen. Having a conference with your team beforehand to strategise is always a good plan.

- Make sure you are happy with the team you have around you and you are comfortable enough to ask any question you like without feeling embarrassed. This is your case, you should be in charge in that respect. This team is working for you.

> *Keep the house and buy your estranged partner out, or you both sell the house and potentially buy another with any equity you are entitled to.*

10

THE HOUSE BUYING PROCESS

Houses: The Good, the Bad and the Ugly…

Once you have your adviser, you will then need to decide on what you are going to do about your marital home. There are normally two options: keep the house and buy your estranged partner out, or you jointly sell the house and, potentially, each buy another with any equity you are entitled to.

Keeping the House

In almost all circumstances, one party must be removed from the mortgage and therefore off the title of the property (deeds). This is called a transfer of equity. There are considerations with this - you would have to be able to afford any new mortgage on your own, and this would include the current mortgage balance, plus any further monies you may have to raise against the property to buy your estranged partner out, if there are no additional funds to do so. This is not always feasible if you have not been the main breadwinner or both incomes were needed to pay the existing mortgage.

Sometimes an agreement can be reached where both parties remain on the title and mortgage until a later date, such as a child reaching age 18, at which point it is written that the property then has to be sold for your ex-partner to be released from the property. In essence, they are agreeing to remain on the deeds of the house and support this until such time any child/children are no longer dependant.

If you decide you can afford a new mortgage on your own, you complete a re-mortgage in your sole name, with the acting conveyancer who is provided by the mortgage lender, completing the transfer of equity, which is the legal process to remove the exiting party from the property deeds. For any other formal arrangement where both parties remain on the property, your family solicitor will be involved in drafting paperwork.

Selling the House

This is an option that gives both parties a clean break. It involves working out any equity within the property (which is the difference between the value of the property and any outstanding mortgages and or loans secured against the property) and agreeing a split of said equity. When doing do, other factors should also be considered such as conveyancing solicitor fees for selling (not the family solicitor), estate agents fees, early repayment charges and mortgage fees. The equity that is then left needs to be agreed upon as a split which isn't necessarily always 50/50.

This is where your family solicitor will be involved in negotiating for you. In terms of getting a sensible valuation, it is advisable to get three different local estate agents round to ensure you are happy with the price point your house will be marketed at and the estate agent you will be working with.

Once the house is sold your share of the equity is then your deposit on your next property, with a mortgage to fund the rest (if needed).

Buying a House

Let's make that lump sum of equity work for you. Once you have spoken with your mortgage adviser, confirmed what you can afford, and have an agreement in principle, it is time to get on *Rightmove* and start searching. You also need to ensure you get registered with all the local estate agents and tell them what you are looking for and what you can afford. Estate agents call their registered buyers before they put properties online and you want to make sure you are one of those registered buyers to be first in the queue to view!

Once you start viewing properties and find that one for you, it is time to make an offer.

Once You've Found Your New Home

Congratulations, your offer is accepted!

The first thing you need to do is choose your conveyancing solicitor. As with most professionals needed in the divorce process, it is a good idea to ask for recommendations from friends, family and colleagues. Some estate agents can help by making recommendations but do check out whether they receive a commission for doing so. A good conveyancing solicitor can impact the speed at which you move into your home, although delays may not necessarily be down to your lawyer!

Next, if you need a mortgage, start your mortgage application. It will need to be accompanied by supporting documents, which may already have been collected by your broker. However, if it is some time since the agreement in principle was carried out, these may need to be updated.

Some of the documents that are likely to be required:

- ID – Personal and address (usually your passport and driving licence)

- Last three payslips (including at least one showing bonuses declared)/Latest accounts/SA302s for the last three years)

- Last 12 months of bank statements showing mortgage or rent being paid out and income being paid in

- Confirmation of any other income such as maintenance payments, child benefit, universal credit.

Mortgage lenders will often ask for additional items once they have received the full application and have begun what is called underwriting. During the underwriting process, the mortgage lender will check that the information you have provided in the application has been confirmed in the supporting documents. They are looking to make sure that you look like someone who will repay the mortgage loan to them, essentially assessing their risk.

Surveys

At this stage, you will need to choose the type of survey or valuation you want. There are three levels available: from the basic one, required by the mortgage lender with their chosen surveyor, to the full building survey, usually carried out by a surveyor selected by you. Your mortgage adviser will talk you through the options, along with the pros and cons and the relative costs.

The mortgage is not just based on whether you are a suitable candidate but also whether the property is good security for the loan. This means they will employ a surveyor to check that the property is valued reasonably, that it is in good order and that there are no obvious structural issues they should be concerned about. It is not an in-depth survey.

This survey is not done for you as a buyer and so shouldn't be relied upon to tell you about any possible concerns in the condition of the property.

The outcome of the mortgage survey can be:

- We're happy to go ahead and lend the amount applied for.

- We're happy to go ahead but there is some remedial work that needs to be done so we'll ask for some specialist reports to be done, such as a damp proof or wall ties specialist or similar. They may hold some money back until the work is completed (known as a retention). Your broker will help you through this and it may mean that you can try to renegotiate the price of the property you are purchasing.

- We're not happy to lend on the property. If this is the case, you might be unhappy but if the surveyor feels it does not provide good security, it might be difficult to sell in the future and you are as well to know early on!

You may wish to consider also paying for an independent, comprehensive survey to ensure you are aware of any remedial work which the property may need. The cost of rectifying any defects could potentially be used to renegotiate the price which you pay for the property.

Legal Work

Once the mortgage company is happy with the survey, they will get on with the mortgage offer. In the meantime, the conveyancing solicitor will be looking through the legal documents that they will receive from the seller's solicitor. They will check the information provided and may need to ask some questions about what they find, known as enquiries. These often relate to rules about things that you can and can't do on your land, known as covenants, such as keeping livestock, allowing people to walk across it because of a right of way or not putting up signage.

Once your lawyer is happy that they have all the information they need, and have received the mortgage offer, they will write a report on title to you and the lender. As long as you and the lender are happy, they will discuss exchange and completion dates with the seller's solicitor.

The exchange of contracts date is the date from which you are legally bound to buy the property, which means that you can be sued if you pull out. The amount quoted is usually ten percent of the purchase price.

The completion date will be set when you exchange and is commonly a week after exchange, although it is becoming more common to have both happen on the same date.

In terms of timescales, this can vary massively - from offer to completion can be eight to twelve weeks but can be outside of these parameters too. Exchange of contracts is the point you sign your life away and completion is the moment you get your keys!

So, What's Next?

What does happen next? Well, once you have that quality mortgage adviser in place, all that is left for you to do is get the paint samples out, have a good look on the *John Lewis* website, and pour yourself a glass of *Amarone*.

Let them do the hard work and you go get excited about your new life in your home!

TAKEAWAYS

- Work out whether one of you can keep the family home or you need to sell it
- Understand the house buying process
- Choose the right survey for you
- Go on recommendations for your conveyancing solicitor
- Make friends with the local estate agents!

> *We are subconsciously taking on the views and actions of those around us... our attitudes towards money have been formed in our heads by the age of seven!*

11

DESIGNING YOUR NEXT CHAPTER (HOW TO THINK ABOUT MONEY)

What is money?

Before we start planning your new life, we need to define money and work out how to think about it. In its simplest terms, money is a medium of exchange, something we can swap for skills or goods.

When we hear of people wanting to win the lottery, it is the things it allows them to have or do that they crave, rather than the money itself. There are people who want to watch their wealth grow for the sake of having money, but for most of us, having money enables us to have the things we would like or do the things we want. It can also buy us freedom from reliance on others, such as employers, customers or a partner, and gives us choices. However, it cannot buy us happiness.

In this chapter, we will start to think about what is important to us and what will bring happiness and contentment.

Money Mindsets

The way you feel about money impacts the way in which you behave with it and can affect what happens when you have it. Do you feel financially secure, and that money is abundant? Or do you feel that there is never enough? I am not asking whether you have overflowing money jars or a million pounds in the bank. This is about how you feel about money, rather than how much you have.

Your money habits, and you will have them even if you weren't the person who looked after the money in your relationship, stem from your mindset. We are all impacted by those around us. We are subconsciously taking on the views and actions of those around us, so that our attitudes towards money have been formed in our heads by age seven! You will have been told things about money as a child. Think about the earliest memory that you have about money. Perhaps it was being given a pound and being told, "Don't spend it all at once". Or maybe it was a relative giving you some coins and saying, "Our secret". Many of us are told that we have to work hard for money, or that if we work hard, we will get more money. Think about the money stories that you tell yourself and whether they serve you well. If they don't, maybe it is time for a change.

Let's look at the two extremes, scarcity and abundance. If you live in a scarcity mindset, you will feel that whatever you do and however much you earn, there is never enough. You are constantly trying to work out how to earn more, keep more, reduce bills and yet there never seems to be enough for the things you want.

In an abundance mindset, you appreciate what you have and enjoy being generous with others. You have confidence in your ability to make money and receive it. You feel confident with money and can take control of it.

You can move from the feelings of scarcity around money to the feelings of abundance, if you are not there already. Your money mindset can be altered when you know where it comes from. The starting point is to recognise it. If you would like to change your attitude towards money, check out our website www.yourdivorcehandbook.co.uk for our FREE guide with some simple exercises to help you to begin to move towards abundance!

How to design your new life

Now you are hopefully feeling more positive around money, let's begin to think about how you would like your life to look. I would strongly suggest a notebook for this section! This is partly because I love a new notebook, but I also think that it's worth doing this comprehensively and writing it all down.

What don't I want?

Many of us find it easier to think about what we don't want than what we do. For example, I know that I don't want to live in a town or city, but I also know that I don't want to live too far away from my children. This gives an area to start looking in. This doesn't just work for location, because you may be very happy where you are, but for all aspects of your life. You might not want to live in a flat, or a house, or a bungalow. You might not want a garden, or a yard. The things you don't want can begin to shape the look of the things that you do.

What do I want to do?

Start to think about what you want to fill your days doing. Do you need to work? If so, do you love your job? Do you feel fulfilled? If not, what else could you do? Do you need training for you to move to a different vocation? Could you set up your own business and do you want to? Would you be able to earn the level of income you need? We spend so much of our lives working. Our work should fulfil our purpose, keep us motivated, bring us satisfaction and preferably joy.

What does retirement look like?

If you are retired, how do you spend your time? Are there other things you would like to be doing? There are lots of clubs, volunteering opportunities, adult learning and more that you can get involved in. If you aren't retired yet, what would you like to spend your time doing when you do finish working? One of my clients wants to spend his time detailing cars, having worked in the law. Another would like to repair and build dry stone walls, having worked in the investment industry.

What about location, do you like where you live? Would you like to travel, to buy a little cottage by the sea, a holiday home, a camper van or enjoy a round-the-world cruise?

What do you want to do for others?

It is also worth considering what you would like to do for others. Do you have a desire to provide house deposits and weddings for your children? What about your parents; are they likely to require financial support? Additionally, are there charities or other good causes that you would like to be able to donate to or, alternatively leave a legacy to in your will?

Bucket List

Finally, consider your bucket list. What are the things that you are absolutely set on doing before you are physically or mentally unable to? This may be visiting a particular place, eating in a particular restaurant, sky diving, bungee jumping, white water rafting, learning to speak a language or to play a musical instrument.

Costing Your New Chapter

You should now have a picture of what you would like your life to look like. The next stage is to get some figures on what this life would cost. Some of the things you want to do won't have a cost, but a lot will. You need to have a clear understanding of the money you need. You can think of this in four parts; the money you need to live your lifestyle while you're working, the money you need to live the life you want to when you are in active retirement, the money you need to live when you are in later retirement and the money you need for the added extras (house deposits, BIG trips and so on come in this category).

When you are planning the next chapter of your life and thinking about the life you want, there are three main levers that you have available to help you to make a plan that really works:

- Earn more
- Work for longer
- Prioritise

Are You Earning Enough?

Now think about your earnings. Do you have enough coming in to support your current lifestyle, save for your desired retirement and for the added extras? You may already have savings, investments and pensions, either that you have saved yourself, inherited or as part of the divorce settlement. You should take these into consideration when you are looking at planning how much you need.

Pay Rise

If your income is not enough, what are the ways of earning more? You might be able to ask for a pay rise. Do you do extra things that are not part of your job role? Write them all down and ask for a meeting with your line manager to discuss a salary increase.

Promotion

You could look to apply for a promotion. It may be that there are opportunities within the business you work in but if not, you can always apply elsewhere. Begin by speaking to your boss to see what other positions might be available to you or look around at other positions. You may need additional training. Start to look at how you can gain the skills that you would need.

Side Hustle

One thing that is becoming very popular is to have a side hustle. This is where you earn extra income outside of your main job. There are lots of ideas online. These may be something like selling on eBay or Etsy, or they could be teaching your hobby, such as yoga or art. For many people, they are keen for their side hustle to become their main job in the future, but it doesn't have to be the case.

Retraining

You may feel that you have always wanted to work as a plumber or electrician or suchlike. You could go back to college to get the training to allow you to do so. Alternatively, you may want to add additional qualifications to enable you to earn more, if you are self-employed. For example, if you are a coach, you might study neuro-linguistic programming, which gives you an additional potential income stream.

If you are considering retraining, it is a good idea to do your sums to work out whether the additional income that you might generate will be worthwhile in comparison with the cost of the training and the time you will need to do it.

Work Longer

Instead of, or as well as, earning more, another option is working for longer. Let's assume that you planned to retire at age 65 but by working until you were 67, you would not have to compromise on any aspect of your life. You might well feel that was worth doing. More and more, we meet people who don't plan to finish working because they enjoy their work and already have a flexible lifestyle. It is hard to believe but retirement was originally only a few short years at the end of our working life. It is only in recent times that we expect to spend the same time, or longer, in retirement.

Prioritise

This is your new chapter that we are designing. So, the final lever is prioritising. This is where you decide that, if doing everything isn't possible, you will choose according to what is most important. For example, if retiring at 60 is really important to you but if you do, the round-the-world cruise is off the table, you then choose which is more important.

Financial Planning

There may be some other ways to increase the money you have available. You could look at tax planning and investing. If you seek advice from a financial planner, they will ensure that they understand the lifestyle that you want to live and then work out the way that you can use what you have, in terms of assets and income, to achieve that life. They may suggest using some tax planning and investment strategies to help you to do so. It is important to take professional advice to ensure that you are doing what is right for you personally, in line with your preferences and attitude to risk.

A financial planner can also hold you accountable if you are looking to save or put money into a pension. You should always leave a planner with a clear picture of your future and the steps you need to take to get there.

I would suggest that you select an independent financial adviser or planner who is not tied to specific products. Whilst advisers are no longer able to be paid for investment advice by commission, it gives peace of mind to know they are selecting what they believe to be the best from the whole market.

No Compromise

The main thing is to enjoy planning your new chapter. Open your mind to a new life, where you can choose the right path for you, with no compromising for someone else. It's also important not to get too attached to your plan because things change in life and in a couple of years, we may see things differently or want different things.

TAKEAWAYS

- Work on your money mindset first
- Use the end of your divorce as an opportunity to design your next chapter, without compromise
- Decide what you want, and more importantly, what you don't want
- Then work out how to get it
- NO COMPROMISING!!

> *A new phase in life
> can open unexpected doors,
> provide previously
> unconsidered opportunities.
> Breathe, and make the
> most of this next phase
> of your journey.*

12

MOVING FORWARD

Starting again after divorce

Setting out in new uncharted waters can mean that life post-divorce seems a daunting prospect. But why not instead breathe and view this as a fresh start, a time to do what you want to do now that you've come through some tough life experiences and have a better awareness of what you want and don't want in your life?

It may take a little time to heal and recover but starting again often prompts reflection on several areas of life.

- **Take time to grieve for your 'old' life**. Many people will offer advice and well-intentioned suggestions, especially if children's lives are to be included in any decision-making. But take time to heal and determine your next step rather than rush into something too hastily.

- **Living arrangements**. It may be that you take things steady by initially choosing to rent rather than buy your next home. Doing that could give time for you to find your feet and reflect on what's best for everyone involved. Some people opt to move to a shared house, which means you have company close by. Do what suits, even if it's going home to Mum and Dad for a while so that you're looked after whilst deciding on your next step.

- **Personal touches** can make a big difference, especially if you're living in temporary accommodation for a while. You may have kept some special items from the marriage, or conversely may have chosen to completely clear out your old life and remove any mementoes. Whatever you decide, personalise your new home, even if it's just a small, short-term let. Source an inexpensive print or two, some lovely cushions, scented candles and turn your personal space into a welcoming haven.

- **Children** may be shared between both parents and it can help them settle by offering them the option to decorate their own bedrooms. It allows them to feel included in the new arrangements, so helping them to move on. Keep channels of communication open for children so they feel able to discuss their feelings.

- **Sometimes a supportive grandparent**, family friend or teacher may be able to provide an outlet for children to talk through their concerns. Be accepting and supportive of that arrangement and understand that they may prefer to talk to a third-party rather than have concerns about worrying you and causing further distress.

- **Social groups** can change significantly post-divorce. Mutual friends may have divided loyalties, feel the new situation is too complicated or be wary that your newly single status will highlight issues in their own relationships. Plus, money and time are often tighter after a divorce, with less disposable income available for socialising, perhaps requiring you to work longer hours or have less free time because of issues with childcare.

- **Work** can become more important after a divorce. Earning money may mean that initially, any convenient job has to be taken. But many people use their divorce as a time to start again. Think about training for something you've always wanted to do or make time for a hobby or interest that you previously felt unable to pursue. When life is already unsettled it can be a good time to use that as an opportunity to introduce something you really want to focus on and develop.

- **How do you feel about yourself**? Divorce can make us feel unloved, unlovable, a failure, guilty at letting others and ourselves down. But the loneliness of a loveless marriage takes its toll and starting again can be a good time for an overhaul to prove to ourselves that we're going to fully invest in our future life. Therapy could play a role in helping you deal with your negative feelings or patterns.

- Could it be time to start eating healthier and lose a few pounds, maybe exercise and start walking, running or going to fitness classes? What about grooming? Going to a different hairdresser or barber may mean you come away with a new look rather than your old familiar style. Makeup counters are often happy to revamp your image and could be a way to get some great new ideas. Be receptive to opportunities for improving your confidence and self-esteem.

- Starting again after divorce can be both scary and exciting. Remember, you're not on your own, so check out local groups that offer things you're interested in. Amateur dramatics, walking, animal welfare, volunteering, night school classes, can all connect you to people with similar interests to yourself.

- Be proactive, find out what's happening locally and organise a social event or two. Be interesting and interested by keeping up to date with national and local news, popular TV, and ensure you're ready to contribute to conversations. That way you'll connect and improve your relationships with others.

Next steps to a new life

Have you ever changed school, moved home, left one job for another and realised that by doing so you're starting again and leaving all your friends behind? Going away to university, getting divorced, moving on, are often exciting times but, nonetheless, can be full of trepidation.

Whilst we may have considered many factors, the impact on our friendship groups may be something we didn't fully appreciate until much later down the line.

Starting again can be an apprehensive time anyway; having to learn where everything is, where we're supposed to be, what we should be doing. There can be a lot to remember and doing these things alone can make everything so much harder. Missing out on having a friendly, familiar face to share a coffee and a chat with can make the first few self-conscious months an awkward and lonely time.

Friends can be a source of comfort and safety, a hug in times of upset. But true friends also care enough to give us a nudge too when needed, encouraging us to move on and keep going, rather than allowing us to feel sorry for ourselves for too long.

Tips for when you're divorced and asking, 'Where are my friends?'

- **A good first step** may be to move into a house share whilst you find your feet. Other occupants may be in a similar position to you and so you're able to provide each other with mutual support. A house share can offer a little security; there's often someone around to talk to, as well as being available for friendship. Or temporarily live with family or friends to ease the financial pressure and provide a temporary buffer.

- **Starting again** can mean that others have already established their friendship groups. If you're the new kid on the block it's important not to appear desperate to make friends. Look after yourself. You may well have been through tough times on your way to starting out afresh or are feeling vulnerable at this unfamiliar situation. The thought of getting up, dressing up and turning up may be daunting.

- **Be kind to yourself** and commit to eating healthily, getting regular sleep and plenty of fresh air. There are times when you've been the newbie before so remind yourself that things do tend to work out fine in the end.

- **Make new friends**. Work, special interest groups, parents' associations can offer convenient ways to meet and connect. But for others, having no friends and starting again requires the effort to be proactive and identify places where kindred spirits may go. Joining a gym, dance class, using public transport, even walking the dog at regular times often means bumping into the same people on a regular basis. A friendly smile or nod of recognition can gradually evolve into a comfortable conversation and potential friendship.

- **Keep in touch** with your old circle of friends through social media, the web, WhatsApp groups and regular calls. Even if doing that makes you feel homesick or is a little upsetting continue with the contact and find ways to remain connected to each other's lives. Maybe schedule a regular call for a proper chat so that you can settle down with a coffee and stay in contact, especially at first.

- **Make invitations**. Take it steady, make an effort and start by suggesting a coffee and a chat. If money is a factor, you could invite them to yours for a bite of supper, pamper evening or games night. Avoid taking rejection personally and instead be interested in getting to know new people, in learning about them and their lives.

- **Gradually familiarise** yourself with what's happening locally. If you hear of something appealing or of general interest why not tentatively suggest an outing to some of your new circle? It's a good way of getting to know people.

- **Accept invitations**. Don't prejudge what you'll like or how you'll feel about 'everyone else'. Go along, relax and be friendly for a few hours in their company doing something different. You may choose to never again repeat the experience, but even so, you've made some new contacts.

- **Ask for help**. It can be tempting to slip into a 'not wanting to be a nuisance or burden' mentality but asking for help can build bridges into new relationships. Remaining private and keeping your insecurities quietly to yourself may be misconstrued as coping, that you're unwilling to share with others or are even unfriendly. Keep your own counsel but also be prepared to connect and let others in.

Starting again can be challenging, but by relaxing, being friendly and interested, it's often enough to ensure that before long you'll have established yourself with plenty of new friends to enjoy.

Is your ex still taking space in your head?

Some people need to allow time to fully recover from their divorce before they can contemplate moving on and dating again. Doing this allows space for valuable lessons to be learned and healing to take place. It can help to avoid rebound situations, where the unrequited love from the previous disastrous relationship is taken and passed onto the next potential love interest.

For some, recovery includes forgiving their ex. Often though, forgiveness is an optional extra. We may not be able to forgive someone's actions, but it's important to forgive ourselves, move on from the relationship and heal any damage done to us.

Let's look at some ways to move on from our ex

- **Understanding what happened** can help. It's often devastating to recall the arguments, the things that were said and done as the relationship was breaking down. Understanding each other's situation can help us move on. Often rows are triggered by stress; business, financial, family, health can all inflame a situation. Things can escalate if they don't feel listened to or understood.

- **Accept responsibility for your own behaviour.** It's rare that one person is good and the other bad. There may well be aspects of your behaviour that you need to learn from. Even if you've tried your very best, done everything, felt that you were being supportive, the situation may have resulted in your ex feeling redundant
  and unnecessary. Or there may have been times when you were perceived as aggressive and your ex felt that they didn't dare speak, learned to keep quiet, but then slowly distanced themselves from the relationship. These insights can help you learn from what went wrong and how to subsequently grow from your divorce experience.

- **Appreciate ways that two people can change** and grow apart over time. If the relationship started when you were very young, your goals and aspirations can evolve differently over time. Other options may come along that offer unexpected opportunities. Or, life can hi-jack your dreams of travelling the world or becoming a best-selling writer. Realism often sets in with the arrival of a mortgage, business commitments, children or elderly parents to consider.

- **Our ex can teach us** about what is really important in life. Through divorce we come to realise what we don't want, but equally what we do want, what matters to us, what our priorities in life really are. Understanding this can enable us to move on from the old, unfulfilling relationship and feel more upbeat about ourselves and our personal options for a more positive future.

All experiences in life have a value. They teach us about ourselves, about others, and about what is important in life. Discovering the best way to move on from a negative relationship, appreciate what we have learned during our time together is a valuable lesson. It forms an important basis for becoming a healthy, viable human being, capable of forming successful future relationships with others.

Or, might there be good reasons to stay friends with your ex?

A break-up is always a challenging time. Often both parties are in very different stages of readiness; one may have been waiting years for the right time to walk away, whilst the other may have felt that things were relatively fine, sticking with the mindset, 'better the devil you know!'

Relationship counselling may have been a valuable way of managing the negative emotions experienced during the break-up of the relationship. It can help with understanding each other's viewpoints, even when the relationship is irretrievable. However, choosing to separate doesn't mean that there aren't good reasons to stay friends with your ex, especially if you've both learned to be more respectful of each other's points of view.

Many practical matters can further exacerbate the situation as they require consideration and can influence decision-making. There's a big list: where to live, the financial implications, custody of family pets, the dispersal of possessions, how to manage the diverse relationships with family and friends, as well as the serious matter of children, their custody, education and the impact a divorce will have on their lives.

Some people say divorce makes them feel a failure; they never envisaged their relationship ending this way. They may feel partly to blame or that they're disappointing their children, family and friends.

Then a reflective period often follows where we consider the many devastating things that have been said and done. We often minimise or even forget the part we played in those heated exchanges. But eventually the hurt and rawness starts to ease and the new life begins.

With that in mind, what are the good reasons to stay friends with your ex?

- **Some couples may have started their relationship** before they'd completed their formal education or become established in their career or business. Over time they've evolved and grown, maybe becoming quite different people. They've shared a lot during through those very personal, early experiences, forming a unique insight and bond.

- **Shared involvement** with children, friends, family, business, may mean that ongoing contact is essential. Making that a courteous, perhaps even pleasant experience reduces stress and is a major reason to stay friendly, if not friends with your ex.

- **Joint counselling** can help improve communications by providing a neutral, safe, supportive environment. Some people have even been known to reconcile as a consequence of improving their ability to listen, empathise and communicate with each other. Whatever the outcome, it can certainly help improve matters.

- **Learning from what went wrong** is an important part of the healing process. Personal counselling can be important to your individual recovery, where you accept responsibility for your role in the break-up and learn ways to avoid repeating negative, unhelpful patterns in future relationships. You may also become more tolerant, understanding and patient of your ex's attitude and decisions.

- **It's important to remember that your ex probably knows you better than anyone** else. Throughout your relationship you've discussed your day-to-day hopes, dreams, fears, issues and concerns, whilst supporting each other with enthusiasm. You used to love each other, laugh together, share your secrets, be part of 'our' team. Breaking up means an end to that intimate day-to-day connection, but your shared history may provide good reasons to stay friends with your ex, even if you're no longer lovers.

- **And, some couples find they get on better after their divorce**. Being removed from their day-to-day arguments, niggles and irritations they can become two separate, independent individuals who may find that they quite like each other and have a lot in common, especially if they share mutual friends, family attachments, work-related interests.

Time apart can enable both of you to become independent and confident about what's right for you, what you need and don't need from a relationship. Having gained valuable insights into yourself and each other there can be good reasons to stay friends with your ex, but in a way that's relevant for today.

The best way to deal with guilt

Many of us feel guilt sometimes in our lives. It may be about the things we've said or done, or even about the things we've missed saying or doing. Guilt is often connected to shame, embarrassment and regret. But long-term, guilt can result in stress and unhappiness. Even health can suffer as a consequence.

- **Is there a repeating pattern** of bad, unfortunate behaviour triggered by certain times or situations? These times can be followed by periods of guilt, contrition and promises to improve. If so, counselling and hypnotherapy are effective ways of addressing and healing negative, destructive behaviour, so allowing a better, more appropriate quality of life to be lived.

- **Accept** that there are times in everyone's life where things occur that we regret. Mistakes happen, we don't always get it right and sometimes say the wrong things. Take responsibility, forgive yourself and apologize, if appropriate. Act quickly, with genuine remorse and then let go of any guilt.

- **Learn** from what's happened. Mistakes can be a powerful way to improve. They teach us about the consequences of our actions, the impact that we can have on others. It's sensible to recognise the value of our experiences and vow not to repeat mistakes, especially relevant if there will be continuing shared points of contact, like children, friends or business connections.

- **Empathy** can be learned as a consequence of guilt. When we recognise that we have hurt another person we can start to appreciate and understand the ways that our actions affect others. We learn about the implications of our behaviour and come to value the importance of thinking before we speak. We hopefully start to consider other people in a more empathic way.

- **Are others trying to make us feel guilty** in a 'don't worry about me, I'll be fine' kind of way? Recognise what others are trying to do and then decide if you're okay with being manipulated in this way. Relatives sometimes try to tug at our heartstrings and make us feel guilty about the break-up. Learn to be firm but kind and explain that they need to accept that you've done what is right for you. Don't allow yourself to be guilt-tripped or forced to explain yourself unnecessarily.

- Mistakes will happen, but being kinder ensures a less judgemental atmosphere, where people become more responsible for their behaviour. They're able to deal with guilt in a humane and understanding way.

When you're ready to join the online dating scene

Modern life has many stresses and pressures. We don't all have the time or opportunity to find a potential new partner as we go about our daily lives. Meeting someone new can be very difficult when you're new to an area, working long hours, newly single or have limited time or money to socialise. Joining a dating site and meeting someone online can be an effective way of getting things started.

Some people have concerns at meeting a new date online and, yes, it is important to be careful about how much information you reveal about yourself, certainly at the outset. Also, some people feel there's no substitute for the frisson of excitement, the chemistry you feel when you first meet someone you're strongly attracted to.

Let's consider the benefits of meeting someone online

- **You can specify the type of person you want to meet**, reveal your interests, the things that you regard as important and let the search criteria do the work for you. Online dating can eliminate weeks and months of going to clubs, bars, gyms hoping to meet someone, when he or she may be just around the corner.

- **You're able to tailor your search** to suit your personal preferences. Music, age range, location, pet lover, smoker or non-smoker can all be specified, all the things that may take a long time to discover if you met someone in person. Yes, you might compromise and be prepared to share their interests if it was someone you really liked, but important differences can become divisive and make you incompatible.

- **It's easy to share personal information** quickly and get to know each other well, before you even agree to meet in person. Communicating online, sharing phone calls means that you have time to think about what you're going to discuss in advance, very different than if you met face-to-face.

- **Because physical intimacy is not such a ready option** it means that online discussions become more in-depth. There's more effort made to have interesting conversations, to form a picture of what each other is like, to learn about each other's views and opinions, to share more than automatic daily updates and gossip. Yes, lighter conversations also happen, but getting to know someone online involves being more focussed on developing the relationship until you agree to meet.

- **It's good to be able to reply to introductions in your own time**, share your thoughts and feelings from the comfort of your own home. Meeting someone in person would be unlikely to include a 'tell me about your childhood/home life/work/past relationships' conversation. Done online, in private, at a time to suit, allows each person to give their full attention to the other, often resulting in sharing personal details that may have never been disclosed before.

Things to remember about online dating

Paying attention to personal safety is an important consideration, so when going to meet someone for the first time it's crucial to follow these basic guidelines; after all, you only know what you've been told online.

Go to the first date in your own car so that you can leave when you want. Agree to meet in a public place, as it's safer and set a time limit of an hour or two in case you feel uncomfortable or sense there's no chemistry. Take your mobile phone and maybe have a friend call after an hour to check that you're okay and give you a 'get out' option. Trust your gut; if you feel uneasy or unsure don't agree to anything that doesn't feel right.

And then you can relax. Take the opportunity to go online and enjoy meeting new friends and potential love interests.

Tips to help you move on from divorce

Moving on can seem daunting, especially if there are outstanding legal and financial matters. There is often personal and emotional readjustment to consider too, usually when we're feeling at our lowest ebb.

- Self-esteem and confidence often suffer as a consequence of divorce, maybe through feeling a failure or concern at letting yourself or others down. Counselling and hypnotherapy can help with processing what went wrong, learn from the experience and become more positive and confident, perhaps even better than before! Addressing unhelpful, underlying patterns and behaviours can help you move forward from your divorce. Healing in part is about dealing with unwanted, negative patterns in order to avoid repeating them in the future.

- Now's the time to become more independent and self-sufficient. Couples often share friends, social interests and decision-making, so moving on alone can feel scary. Include friends and family, take things at your pace, adopt a realistic perspective, laugh at your mistakes and make the transition easier. Accept that in relationships there are often his and her tasks. You may need time to learn to do things you've never done before. Ask for help, let go of frustrations and be gentle with yourself. It can take time to move on!

- Aim to keep yourself relevant and up-to-date. Keep in touch with the outside world and stay connected. Watch the news and popular TV so that you can join conversations. Invest in your appearance, even if it's a simple colour change or gentle makeover. Plan a pamper evening, supper party, card evening or watch the match. Play board games together, all fun, easy ways to keep in touch. Let others contribute a dish or bottle so it costs little.

- Home may feel very different post-divorce. It may be time to relocate and focus on establishing a new home for you and yours. Or financial considerations may make selling the marital home prohibitive for the time being. Staying there may be viable in the short-term; it allows time to settle, heal and plan ahead. If so, find ways to reorganise your home. Rugs, prints and little touches can make a real difference. Let the children help so that they feel involved and invested too.

- Possessions can be a tough call. Often getting rid of things can be both symbolic and cathartic. Sometimes letting something go that meant a lot can be the right thing to do. Do you really want to be reminded of your relationship every time you enter a room?

- Sleeping alone may feel strange at first. Change your mindset about your bedroom - it's your place now. Turn it into a haven and put lavender on your pillow, take a relaxing bath and get cosy in your space.

- Earning money may be extra important so there's a requirement for you to settle down to work and commit to your job or career. Or could now be time to start out again and achieve something you've always wanted to do, something special, that's all yours? Re-write your CV, investigate career options or re-training. Consider the best way to make that fresh start and look at a new career or starting a business of your own. This could be your catalyst for change!

As you find your feet appreciate the opportunity for a new beginning and discover positive ways to move on from your divorce.

Take a few moments to reflect on those times in life when you've had to start again and dig deep to find both the strength and resilience to carry on. The first day at school, at college, starting a new job, moving away from home, going on a first date; all these are typically times filled with trepidation, times that can be daunting, unnerving and filled with promise, all at the same time.

It's what you do during and after your divorce that counts. Let it count for something and set the tone for a fulfilling next stage of your life. As you find your feet appreciate the opportunity for a new beginning and discover positive ways to move on from your divorce.

TAKEAWAYS

- Allow yourself time to grieve and heal; endings need time to recover

- Take responsibility for your part in what's gone on and gone wrong

- This is a fresh start, a time to right wrongs & move forward. Allow that to happen.

- Do you have to finish with your relationship completely? Is friendship an option?

- Take other people's advice with caution. Following it leaves you and not them with the consequences!

THE STORY AND PEOPLE BEHIND THE BOOK

In late 2020, in the midst of the global Covid-19 pandemic, I brought together a group of Family Law professionals to help and support local people, to be known as the South Manchester Family Group. The group was formed to provide support to one another in our specialist areas and to our clients. Due to the extended use of video conferencing by this time, we began to work with clients across the UK. At the beginning of 2021, we launched a Facebook group, Separation, Divorce and Dissolution UK, to additionally support these people. The Facebook group has been a great success and gave us an awareness of the huge need for information. In May 2021, I floated my idea of a book past the divorce team, and it was enthusiastically received. We very much hope that you found it useful.

Let us now introduce ourselves:

Tamsin Caine is a Chartered Financial Planner and Resolution Accredited Divorce Specialist. She divorced herself in 2017. That, along with her experience of her parents' divorce as a teenager, set her on a path to help those going through separation, divorce or civil partnership dissolution. In 2018, she founded Smart Divorce with an aim to help more people split up amicably and come to settlements without the need for court. She helps both couples (as a financial neutral) and individuals to negotiate sorting out their finances through various stages of the divorce process, supporting them and holding their metaphorical hand. Whilst she is based in South Manchester, she works with clients across England and Wales.

Outside work, Tamsin is mum to Charlie and Zoe. She is a huge rugby union fan, supporting Sale Sharks and Sale FC, where she has volunteered for the past eleven years. She also loves baking, reading and is working on her photography skills, particularly during one of her regular hikes in her beloved Peak District.

Susan Leigh is a counsellor, hypnotherapist, relationship counsellor, writer & media contributor based in South Manchester. She offers help with relationship & divorce issues, stress management, assertiveness and confidence. She works with individual clients, couples and provides corporate workshops and support.

She is the author of three books, *Dealing with Stress, Managing Its Impact, 101 Days of Inspiration #tipoftheday* and *Dealing with Death, Coping with the Pain,* all on Amazon with easy-to-read sections, tips and ideas to help you feel more positive about your life.

Early mornings, Susan can be found walking the banks of the Bridgewater Canal, taking photos, which are a source of joy and inspiration to many of her followers.

Marcia Lister, a pioneer for mediation since commencing legal practice over 20 years ago. Marcia has worked exclusively as an independent mediator since 2004 and founded her own practice Marcia Mediation Limited in 2013.

Whether mediating cases involving high conflict child disputes or any kind of financial and property disputes, Marcia's approach is to promote a forward-looking approach to resolution by focussing on what can be agreed rather than what cannot. Building from there, Marcia is known for her proactive approach to the process which has allowed her to broaden her remit to cases involving the wider family, including grandparents and even to disputes involving wills and probate where similar principles work well.

Marcia's clients are encouraged to avoid the cost, stress and uncertainty of the court procedure and empowered to craft an agreement which whilst it cannot give them both what they want, will give them both what the need to move forward without recrimination, with dignity and readier to face the challenges of the new start ahead.

Marcia is married with two grown up sons. When not working, she loves nothing more than long country walks with her cocker spaniel Murphy.

Katie McCann is a family lawyer and barrister, specialising in assisting couples to separate in the best way possible for them and their families. Her main area of focus is achieving sensible financial settlements for her clients. She has acted for clients from all sections of society, from multi-millionaires and celebrities, through to the local police officer trying to protect their pension. She prides herself on treating every client with the respect and care they need on this section of their journey and believes in dealing with each case and its unique facts with pragmatism and realism. She is the owner of her own family law boutique brand Lowry Legal.

Katie is someone who loves a challenge! She has taken part in a charity *Strictly Come Dancing* competition, dancing the Paso Doble. During lockdown, she has raised money for charity doing a virtual duathalon. She is a massive fan of fitness and taking care of her general all round wellbeing. She is on the lookout for her next fitness challenge which looks set to be an international bike ride for "Parkinsons UK", a charity close to her heart.

Carole Nettleton qualified as a solicitor in 1996 and has practised exclusively in Family Law since then working in Liverpool and Manchester city centre firms and is now based at Price Slater Gawne in Altrincham, South Manchester.

She has extensive experience dealing with divorce, dissolution of civil partnership and the breakdown of cohabitation with the associated consequences of relationship breakdown.

Her area of expertise includes dealing with the finances of high-net-worth individuals and also cases where assets are more modest but frequently, her cases will involve complex pension issues, multiple businesses, confiscation proceedings and family trusts.

Carole also deals with private children matters ranging from the time children spend with parents to more complex issues of taking children to live in another country.

Outside of work Carole enjoys running, racquet sports, music, BBC Radio 4, spa days, podcasts and cricket (having two boys who play and talk about cricket non-stop).

Daniel Bell has always been a numbers enthusiast and has always loved finance. Even before leaving school, he knew that working with money, finance and numbers was going to feature large in his future aspirations.

He started work in the world of banking, progressing to Branch Manager, before leaving to become a financial adviser. For him building personal relationships with clients has always been the key, loving the role he has in people's lives, dispensing advice that supports them at different stages of their decision-making. Trust, integrity and good quality client care are the foundation upon which he's built his reputation and his business, each relationship individually tailored to suit the particular client.

Away from the calculator, he is married to Sam who also works in the business, and they share their home with George the Pug. Socialising in the city, exploring in the country and living for tomorrow, that's how he rolls. Certainly, a 'life is too short' philosophy and therefore he's the life and soul of the party too!

ABOUT THE COVER

Have you heard of Kintsugi? It's a Japanese technique for mending broken pottery by pouring gold, silver or platinum into any cracks and breaks, making even ordinary objects whole, and often more beautiful than before.

It celebrates the journey that the object has been on, rather than try to disguise or conceal it.